Silicon
and the
Single
Bookseller

by

Peter A McWilliams

Prelude Press

Preface

This book is for two kinds of booksellers:

1. The bookseller who may be considering the purchase of a small computer for his or her bookstore.

2. The bookseller who must sell computer books, but is wondering, "What *are* those television-typewriters anyway?"

For the second group of booksellers, this book will tell you, as painlessly as possible, what personal computers are, what they do, what they don't do, and provide a crash course in Conversational Computerese along the way. The next time a thirteen-year-old walks into your store and asks for a book on 8080 chips, or a rep tries to sell you a book on CP/M, you'll know what they're talking about.

For the owner of a personal bookstore contemplating the purchase of a personal computer, this book is the first word, not the last, on the subject.

The ABA has taken upon itself the monumental task of evaluating the computing needs of small bookstores. Their booklets, "ABA Computer Specifications for Independent Bookstores" and "ABA Evaluation of Computer Hardware & Software Vendors," are of great value to booksellers with RAMs in their eyes.

This book is not designed to replace those booklets. If anything, this book is designed to make those booklets more useful.

This book will offer some suggestions on how to buy a computer, and a few frank comments on which computer to buy.

It is not necessary to get a computer for your bookstore that does everything a computer *can* do. Maybe getting a computer to do the few things your store needs most would be less complicated—and less expensive.

Word processing and basic accounting (accounts payable, accounts receivable, etc.) are, for example, relatively straightforward and cost effective, while precise inventory control tends to be more expensive and time consuming.

This book was pilfered from "The Personal Computer Book," "The Word Processing Book," and "Questions and Answers on Word Processing." ("The Personal Computer in Business Book" was still, as they say in computing, in process, or, as they say in publishing, not available at press time.)

The excerpts have been selected and arranged to be of maximum value to all booksellers, be they sellers of computer books or potential computer owners.

Before we continue, a personal note: I have made my living in publishing, thanks to booksellers, for the past sixteen years. This book is, more than anything else, an expression of my gratitude.

Here we have an early personal computer on the left and an early word processor on the right. It's hard to believe that no one thought of putting the two together until the last quarter of the Twentieth Century

The Pharaoh's daughter finds a word processor floating in the stream.

Introduction

This is a book for people who know little or nothing about computers, personal or otherwise.

It's for people who have had their curiosity piqued by the televised endorsement of computers by such diverse personalities as Dick Cavett, George Plimpton, and Charlie Chaplin. It is a book for those who, watching these commercials, have asked themselves, "Dick Cavett?" "George Plimpton?" *"Charlie Chaplin?"*

It's a book for those who wonder what personal computers are, what they have to offer, and what these offerings will cost.

It's for people who have had their "computer literacy" questioned by such literary giants as *Time, Newsweek,* and *People.*

It's for people who don't know the difference between a microprocessor and a microorganism — who think a "Pac-Man" is a member of the Sierra Club.

Finally, and most importantly, it is a book for people who aren't all that serious about the whole computer thing. I am reminded of the late Alan Watts, who said that he was not *serious* about his work, but that he was *sincere.* I am sincere in my admiration of personal computers as powerful tools, and I am sincerely amused by those who take these tools too seriously.

In researching this book, it was necessary to attempt reading the other introductory books on personal computers. One claimed that computers were the most important invention since fire, or perhaps the wheel. I only got through three or four more pages of that book. Another said that computers were the most important step, evolutionwise, since our ancestors jumped out of the trees. I stopped reading that one right there.

Having, in my own haphazard way, studied computers for three years — and having owned a personal computer for two — I find it difficult to accept as a guide anyone that *serious* about computers.

In this book I will do my best to be a sincere guide, though not a serious one.

Taken from "The Personal Computer Book."

If I were to look upon the time line of humanity, and were asked to locate an evolutionary turning point that most closely resembles the advent of personal computers, I wouldn't have to go back any farther than thirty years — the popular acceptance of television. Television was successfully demonstrated in 1927 and made commercially available in 1941, but it wasn't until the late 1940s and early 1950s that television became truly popular. (In 1946 there were 10,000 TVs in the United States. By 1951 there were 12,000,000. In 1958 — 50,000,000.)

Few will deny the impact television has made upon the United States and most of the industrialized world. Observing us coolly from North of the border, Canadian philosopher Marshall McLuhan noted that the world had become a global village.

I do not think, however, that television rates the same niche in the evolution of the species as fire or learning to walk on two legs. Nor do personal computers.

As with all the technological advances of the last hundred years — typewriters, telephones, electric lights, phonographs, automobiles, airplanes, movies, radio, television — personal computers will change our lives, and our lives will change them.

In some areas, personal computers will prove so invaluable that they will soon be considered a necessity — small businesses for example. Big business simply could not continue without their big computers. (It is estimated that duplicating the daily output of all the large computers in the world would require three *trillion* clerical workers.)

Word processing, accounting, cost projections, inventory control, and similar functions are handled so swiftly and effortlessly by personal computers that, within a few years, the small businessperson will be as addicted to small computers as the big businessperson is addicted to the big. (See the chapter on *Personal Computers in Business*.)

In other areas, personal computers will prove so unnecessary as to be considered a nuisance — reading the daily newspaper, scheduling appointments, filing personal income taxes, locking the doors at night, or turning the coffee on in the morning.

In most areas, however, true to its name, the value of a personal computer will depend upon the personal interests of the person using the computer. Personal computers play games — from chess to Missile Command —better than anything else around. But you must fancy games. They will chart your biorhythms with great accuracy. But you must care to know what your biorhythms are. Using a telephone to plug into a large computer, you can research any subject imaginable. But first, you must have something to research.

For the most part, personal computers will prove their worth to the degree that they fit into your daily life, not to the degree that you adapt your life to be more in step with The Computer Age.

In this book, we'll explore the things that personal computers do — the things they do well and the things they don't do well. You can decide if any of these accomplishments warrant inviting this latest prodigy of the industrial revolution into your home or office.

COMPUTERS BY BALLOON.

The Personal Computer

Before exploring what these E.Ts. called P.Cs. do, let's take a look at what they *are*.

Like most machines, personal computers are made up of metal, glass, paper, and plastic — with an occasional exotic-sounding substance like phosphorus thrown in for good measure.

If you feel intimidated by computers, there's no need to be. They are constructed of the same bits and pieces as televisions, typewriters, and tape recorders.

This chapter will provide a general overview of a personal computer's component parts. We'll go into more detail, from a buyer's point of view, in a later chapter, *Selecting a Personal Computer*.

As we go along, I will also introduce you — as painlessly as possible — to that collection of jargon, technical terms, and buzz words known as **Computerese**. There's nothing to be intimidated about here, either. The people who created Computerese are far less intelligent than you. How do I know they are far less intelligent than you? Because, considering the mishmash of tortured conjunctions and fractured idioms they have jumbled together, it's obvious that they are far less intelligent than anyone.

And so, with intimidation on hold, heads held high, and a song in our hearts, let's take a look at the bits and pieces that make up a personal computer.

The first bit of the personal computer we'll look at is the **microprocessor**. A processor in *any* computer does just that: it **processes** information. It sorts and resorts bits of information, something almost any human could do, but it sorts and resorts at speeds no human can approach. It is this speed, not any innate ability, that give computers the edge over humans in certain repetitive tasks.

In a larger computer, the processor can be any size at all. A large corporation can simply lease another floor to put it on. In a personal computer, a processor can be only so large or it stops being a personal computer and

Taken from "The Personal Computer Book."

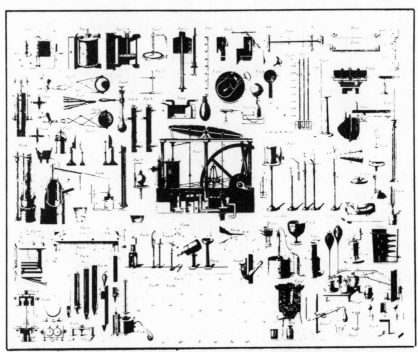

The component parts of a personal computer (PLATE 1).

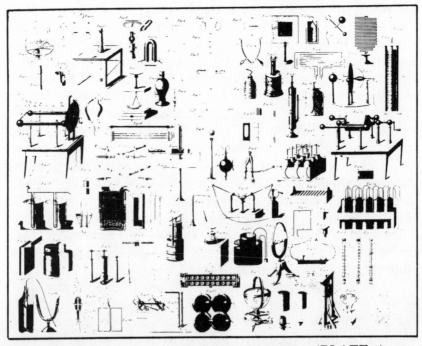

The component parts of a personal computer (PLATE 2).

becomes a coffee table. Once processors became small enough they were dubbed *micro*processors. (In the world of electronics, when something is made small it is prefaced with *mini*. When it is made smaller it is prefaced by *micro*, and when it is made smaller still, by *mini-micro*. I am sure before the decade is out we will see *micro-micros*, *mini-micro-micros*, and *micro-micro-micros*.)

Some microprocessors are basic affairs, designed for a specific function within a specific product. A microprocessor inside a hand-held calculator, for example, may be constructed to simply add, subtract, tell the time, and play a heart rending version of *Clair de lune*.

By the time they mature enough to be included in a personal computer, microprocessors assume the more sophisticated name of **Central Processing Unit**, which is usually shortened to the not-so-sophisticated **CPU**.

Microprocessors are made of silicon. Silicon is a fancy word for glass. (Not to be confused with *silicone*, a fancy word for rubber.) It's called silicon because it is made from silica, a fancy word for sand.

It has been said that the meek shall inherit the earth. Remember those meek little math students, running around high school with slide rules and pencils sticking out of their shirt pockets, the ones the jocks labeled nerds, the ones who never dated because (a) no one would date them and (b) they were always in the basement working on their science project? Well, those meek have inherited the earth, the sand to be specific, silica to be more specific.

They have inherited, too, a chunk of actual earth in California called Silicon Valley (not to be confused with Silicone Valley, a section of Beverly Hills reserved for plastic surgeons and their more affluent clients). In Silicon Valley the nerds have become rich with their science projects, and the former-jocks all over the country are trying to save enough money to buy one of these mass-produced projects for their children.

A microprocessor is very smart but has very little memory, rather like a genius with amnesia. To remedy this situation, two kinds of memory are combined with the Central Processing Unit in most personal computers.

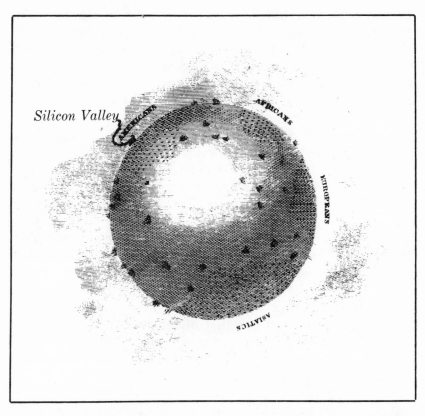

Silicon Valley

The first is known as **Read Only Memory or ROM**. This memory can be "read" by the microprocessor, but the microprocessor cannot "write" anything onto that memory. (*Reading*, meaning taking information from, and *writing*, meaning adding information to, are computerdom's token nods to a form of literacy other than computer literacy.) The microprocessor, then, is free to take information *from* ROM but it cannot add information *to* it.

The information in ROM is placed there — permanently — by the manufacturer. ROM is there like a helpful nurse, telling the amnesia-bound genius how to brush his teeth, get dressed, and otherwise prepare for the day. When electrical current first passes through the CPU, it will wake up and ask ROM, "What do I do now?" ROM will tell it, CPU will do it, and then ask, "What do I do now?" ROM will tell it, CPU will do it, and so on. ROM is, in other words, **programmed** to get CPU going in the morning and to maintain certain basic functions during the day.

At a certain point, however, CPU will have done everything ROM has been programmed to ask it to do. CPU is washed, dressed, and ready for the day — but what will that day consist of? CPU asks ROM, "What do I do now?" and ROM replies, "Ask RAM."

RAM is the second kind of memory in a personal computer. RAM stands for **Random Access Memory**. With RAM, not only can CPU read information from RAM, but it can also write information on it. It has random access to that memory; can erase it — or any part of it — and write some more.

RAM is also referred to as **User Programmable Memory**. This means that the user (you or I) can "program in" whatever we want the CPU to do. (We'll discuss programming a computer in Chapter Three. For now, know that programming RAM is as easy as playing a record on a phonograph.)

The CPU turns to RAM and asks, "What do I do now?" RAM has the daily schedule from the Big Boss (you) in hand. "During the morning it's accounting," says RAM, "This afternoon word processing, and in the evening we have scheduled a series of intriguing electronic games." "Right," says CPU, and the three of them — RAM, ROM, and CPU — set off for a productive day.

RAM can be thought of as an executive secretary who has not only the daily schedule, but also a steno pad. If CPU were to ask ROM to take a note, ROM would reply, "That's not my job. Ask RAM." RAM is more than happy to jot down anything from a telephone number to a telephone book, and to have that information ready for the CPU's use at a nanosecond's notice.

RAM is obviously a more versatile servant to CPU than ROM, but RAM, alas, has a memory problem of its own. As long as electrical current is flowing through its little brain, RAM remembers everything. Once the current is withdrawn, RAM forgets it all. (ROM, on the other hand, remembers how to get CPU up and dressed, current or no current, indefinitely.) Every time a computer is turned

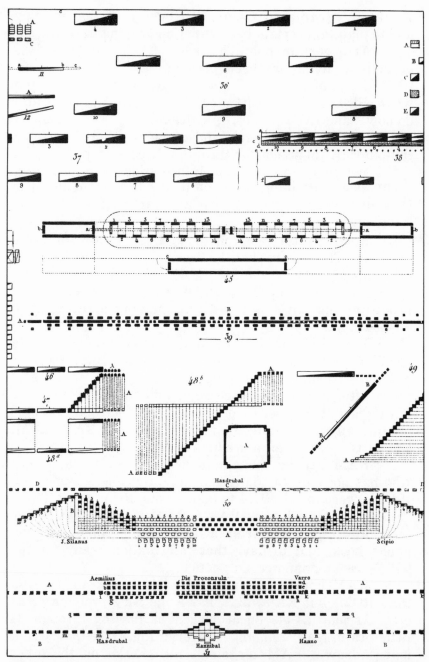

Here we have a diagram of the inner workings of a personal computer.

off, it's a blank tabula rasa for RAM.

There must be a way, then, to (a) save the information in RAM before turning the power off and (b) loading information back into RAM after turning the power back on. That way is either cartridges or magnetic media.

Cartridges look like 8-track tapes and plug into the computer. These can either be game playing cartridges (a different game or set of games on each cartridge), or more "serious" applications — a checkbook cartridge, for example, might keep a running balance of how overdrawn you are.

Magnetic media for personal computers come in two types, tapes and disks. The tapes used are of the standard cassette variety, the same kind you'll find in $4,000 audiophile tape decks, $100 Sony Walkmans, and $19.95 cassette players from K Mart.

Disks are either 5¼- or 8-inch circles of plastic covered with the same brown stuff that is found on cassettes. (The brown stuff, by the way, is rust; ordinary garden-hoe variety rust. Naturally, no one would want to pay $5 for a piece of plastic covered with rust, so the rust is known as "iron oxide.") These thin circles are permanently enclosed in a cardboard envelope to protect them from dust, dirt, and sticky fingers. These disks are also known as **floppy disks**, **minidisks**, and **diskettes**.

Cassettes require nothing more elaborate than the aforementioned $19.95 K Mart cassette player and some sort of interface to work with a personal computer. (An **interface** is any device that lets one device work with another device. Clear?)

Disks require a special player known as a **disk drive**. A disk goes into a disk drive, protective covering and all. There, the inner plastic circle is rotated at several hundred rotations per minute, while a record/playback head moves across the disk's surface. These heads are known as **read/write heads**. Information is read from the disk and written on the disk by them. Most drives have one read/write head, unless it is a **double sided** disk drive, in which case it would have two heads — rather like the old juke boxes that could play either side of a vertically spinning record.

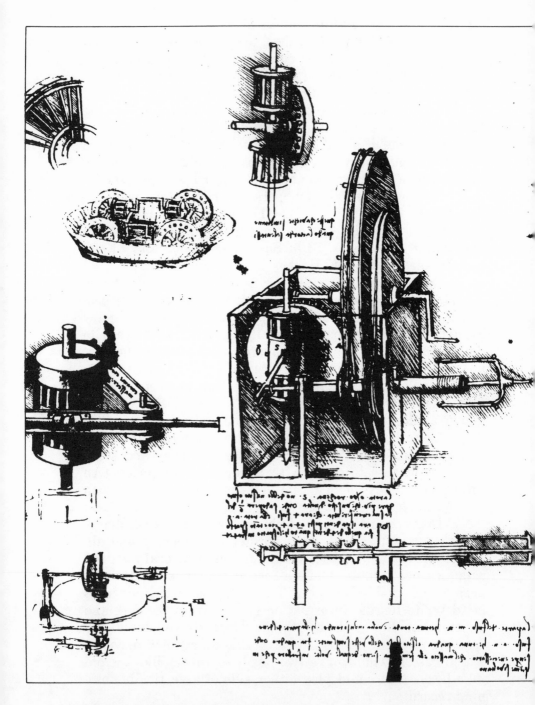

The idea for the disk drive is not new. Here are Leonardo da Vinci's sketches for a manually operated disk drive, circa 1490.

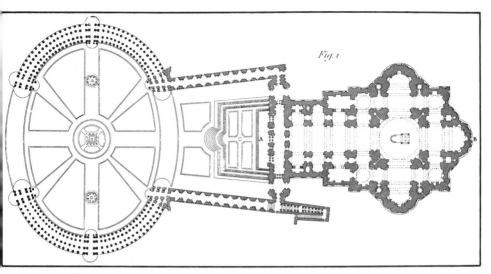

Michelangelo tried to improve upon Leonardo's design by making the disks oval ("More esthetically pleasing," Michelangelo wrote in his journal). Leonardo, in Florence, sent a terse note to the young sculptor in Rome: "Whatsa matta you?" Leonardo wrote, "The diska drive, shesa my idea. You keepa you hands off." Michelangelo eventually found another use for his design.

Early disk drives required one full horsepower to operate.

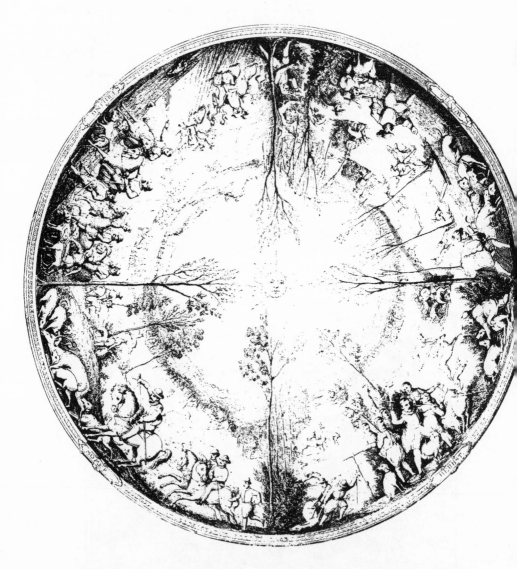

How information is stored on disks: Here we have the disk for the video game "A Weekend in the Country." As you can see, everything is made small so it can fit.

Cassette players, as you may have surmised, are less expensive than disk drives. Cassettes are, however, much slower and far more prone to error. (We'll discuss cassettes vs. disks further in the chapter on *Selecting a Personal Computer*.)

Another kind of magnetic media becoming more and more popular with personal computers, especially personal computers used for business applications, are **hard disks.** Hard disks operate very much like floppy disks. The difference between a floppy disk and a hard disk is that the hard disk is made of metal, not plastic; it spins at a much faster speed; it holds five to fifty times more information; it reads and writes faster; and, of course, it costs more. Whereas floppy disks are changeable, hard disks (usually) are not.

With magnetic media we have a way of getting information into RAM when we turn the computer on, and a way to store information from RAM before we turn the computer off. But how do we get in and fiddle around with the information in between times? What we need are some **input devices.** That's where keyboards and joysticks come in.

A **keyboard** is a board with keys on it, looking very much like the keyboard on a typewriter. Each key represents a letter or a number or a bit of punctuation or a symbol of some kind.

Inexpensive personal computers use **membrane keyboards.** These are flat membranes of rubbery plastic with the keys printed on the surface. When the rubbery plastic is depressed and electrical contact is made just below its surface, a keystroke is recorded.

Less inexpensive personal computers ($300 and up, in most cases) use mechanical keyboards that more closely resemble the action of a typewriter. Each letter, number, or symbol has its own plastic key. This key is attached to an electrical switch. Each time a key is depressed, contact is made, and a keystroke is registered. Mechanical keyboards are much easier to use than are the membrane variety.

With a keyboard, almost anything can be communicated to a computer. Words, numbers, symbols, which way the spaceship should go, when it should fire, and so on. Even graphics can be communicated through the keyboard. (A device known as a **light pen** can also be used. This allows one to draw on the computer screen just as though it were chalk on a chalkboard.)

Serious game players, however, will require a **joystick**. A joystick is a little box one holds in one's hand. A stick protrudes from this box, as do one or more buttons. If one pushes the stick up, the spaceship (or submarine or boxer or chess piece) moves up the screen. When the stick is pushed down, the spaceship *et al* moves down. The same is true of right, left, diagonals, and circles.

When the button is pushed, a missile is fired (or a torpedo is launched, or a punch is thrown, or a move is finalized). All this stick moving and button pushing has been observed to create the emotion of Joy in certain humans, hence the term joystick.

Input devices — keyboards and joysticks — get information into the computer. How do you suppose we get information out? You guessed it: **output devices**. These include video screens and printers.

The **video screen** on a personal computer looks just like the screen on a television set — in fact, the video screen on some personal computers actually *is* a television set. A wire connects the personal computer to the antenna of a television and the computer literally broadcasts a signal to the TV.

A video screen is also known as a **CRT**, which stands for cathode ray tube, which is the kind of tube a TV picture tube really is.

The video screen (or **video display**) of more sophisticated personal computers is not a computer-by-day and a television-by-night. These video screens are known as **monitors** and are connected directly to the computer. Monitors display better images than do moonlighting televisions.

The display can be either in color or **monochrome**. Monochrome simply means "one color." Monochrome colors for personal computers are green (dark green background with lighter green lettering), amber (dark amber background with lighter amber — almost yellow — lettering), and the ever popular white (white lettering against a basic black background.) Most computers allow the screen display to be reversed so that dark characters can appear against light backgrounds.

Color video is everywhere. We're so used to seeing color when we look at a video screen that some advertising agencies, in yet another desperate attempt to attract our attention, are now producing television commercials in black & white. For games, graphics, and the education of younger children, color video is certainly the way to go. For words and numbers, however, monochrome displays offer sharper character display.

Video displays are ephemeral. Like RAM, once the power is turned off, the video screen forgets. A more permanent method of "outputting" information is found in the **printer**. A printer, naturally, prints things.

A printer is known as a **peripheral**. It is so named because it is peripheral to the use of the computer — useful, but not necessary. At one time, almost everything other than CPU, ROM, and RAM were considered peripherals. As personal computers have gotten more sophisticated, the line between "the computer" and "its peripherals" has blurred. Is a disk drive a peripheral? A keyboard? A joystick? People have differing opinions. Most people do, however, draw the line at printers. (An "all in one" personal computer might include everything we've discussed thus far, but would not include a printer.)

There are two kinds of printers, dot matrix and letter quality. **Dot matrix** printers form characters with little dots, very much like the signs on banks that tell the time and temperature. Dot matrix printers are not the greatest for correspondence, but are necessary for intricate graphics.

For correspondence (letters, reports, and such) one would need a **letter quality** printer. These print a bit slower and cost a bit more than their dot matrix cousins, but the quality of their type rivals that of electric typewriters. This is because, in a very real sense, they *are* electric typewriters. They type one character after another, just like a typewriter. Printers made especially for computers are constructed for continual full-tilt use, something most typewriters are not. Further, computer printers are designed to use some features not generally available on typewriters, such as boldface printing.

Another popular peripheral for the personal computer is known as a **modem**. A modem attaches to the computer and to a telephone. It allows one computer to be connected, over phone lines, to another computer. (The other computer requires a modem as well.) When connected, information can flow back and forth between computers.

The process modems use to transmit computer information over ordinary phone lines is called *modulation*. (Modulation also takes place with information before it can be broadcast over the airwaves. The "M" in AM and FM radio stands for modulation.)

A modem takes information from the computer, modulates it, and sends it over the phone line. A second modem at the other end *de*modulates the signal back into a form the receiving computer can understand. "Mo-dem," then, describes what a modem does — *mo*dulate/*dem*odulate.

A modem puts your computer in touch with the world.

*In the 1920s, this was one of radio's most popular "peripherals."
Prior to the loudspeaker, all listening had to be done through
headphones. Considering its potential, personal computing is about
where radio was in the early 1920s.*

Making phosphor.

An Incomplete and No Doubt Inaccurate History of Personal Computers Including Some Basic Information on How They Work

Boy, I sure wish I had Mr. Wizard to help me with this chapter. Somehow Mr. Wizard made "the magic and mystery of science" understandable and, even when it wasn't understandable, at least it was fun.

If this were television, there would be a shot of me, leaning pensively on the edge of my keyboard, saying "Boy, I sure wish I had Mr. Wizard to help me with this chapter," and suddenly Don Herbert would appear, maybe in a white lab coat, maybe in a suit, and I would become Everyperson and he would become Mr. Wizard, and tell us all about how computers work.

Alas, this is not television, this is a book, and nothing appears suddenly during the writing of a book other than creditors. If this book ever becomes a TV show, maybe the budget will permit Mr. Wizard to join us.

It would be nice to have Sir Kenneth Clark of *Civilization* stop by, too. Lord Clark could show us, through the sketches of Michelangelo and the paintings of the Louvre, how computing has developed through the ages. *Computization* we'll call it. Besides, it's always good to have a "Sir" on the show.

Until that time we'll muddle through on our own, knowing that somewhere, somebody must know how to make all this stuff clear.

Taken from "The Personal Computer Book."

This is an optional chapter. You will never need to know *how* computers work. All you need to know is *that* they work. (They do.)

Somewhere along the line you may want to learn how to *operate* a computer, but that is very different from how a computer operates. How a computer operates is of no practical value whatsoever — unless you're a computer designer.

Most of the books and articles written about computers have been written by scientists — or worse, by people trying to *sound* like scientists — and what scientists find necessary to know they assume everyone will find necessary to know. We don't.

How many people know how their refrigerator works? Let's have a show of hands. Your cassette tape recorder? Your car? Your houseplants? Your liver? Does it really matter if you don't? All that matters is that you know how to run it, play it, drive it, water it, or leave it blessedly alone so that it can operate as designed, unmolested.

At some point, even the most educated among us must say, "I don't know how it works" to some essential bit of machinery, and somehow that ignorance doesn't stop the machine from working. Somewhere there is an expert who does know how it works — or at least how to fix it — and that's all that's necessary.

And so it is with computers. That there are silicon chips sorting and re-storing billions of binary bits per nanosecond is of no practical concern to the corporate attorney playing Pac-Man or the teenager using a computer to write his first love poem.

The much-used phrase "computer literacy" has little to do with knowing what goes on inside the machine. It has to do with getting what you want *into* the machine and getting what you want *out of* the machine, and feeling comfortable enough about this process of in and out to occasionally enjoy it.

"Turn the machine on, put the record on the turntable, put the needle on the record, and adjust the volume to your taste" is all one needs to know about a phonograph to enjoy everything from Bette Midler to Gustav Mahler.

The fact that sound is made up of vibrations, and that these vibrations are captured in the grooves of the record, and that the needle vibrates when going through those grooves, and that those vibrations when amplified recreate the original vibrations and therefore the sound of the original performance, is not necessary to know.

It can, however, be interesting. A *National Geographic Special* on how the human body works can be fascinating, even though we've been successfully operating our bodies for years without all those microscopic, time-lapsed, animation-enhanced "hows."

And so it is with the hows, as well as the history, of computers. (The hows and the history of most machinery is intimately connected.) What follows are some hows and some history of computing, presented in no particular order and selected because I found each of them for some reason interesting. This is decidedly not a comprehensive overview of the history and internal functioning of computing machines. It's more a collection of computer trivia.

If your eyes begin to glaze or your mind begins to drift during any of these points, don't bother to refocus and reread, just skip to the next point. If you drift on several points, skip to the next chapter. This information is not in the least essential to selecting, purchasing, operating, and enjoying a personal computer. Like all trivia, it can be interesting but it is, in essence, trivial.

• The first computer was the abacus. The abacus is from the Orient, although its name comes from the Greek word abax, meaning a calculating table covered with dust, which was named after the Hebrew word for dust. The abacus is more than 5,000 years old and is still the primary form of "number crunching" in many parts of the world. (Although the 1982 Chinese census was counted on modern computers, the census preceding it was computed on the abacus.)

The abacus is not only one of humankind's first complex machines, it's also the first mechanical device listed in most dictionaries.

• The next major breakthrough in computers came a scant 4,600 years after the invention of the abacus. In 1642, French scientist Blaise Pascal invented an "arithmetic machine" to help in his father's business. (A father's necessity was the mother of this invention.)

The machine had eight wheels, each wheel having the numbers 0 through 9 painted on them. The wheels were attached to gears and the gears attached to each other in such a way that simple addition and subtraction could take place by dialing the amounts to be added or subtracted. Its size made it the world's first non-portable computer.

Blaise Pascal was honored by having a high-level computer language — Pascal — named after him. (I understand that a low-level computer language, Blaise, is in the works.)

• In 1694, 52 long years after Pascal's arithmetic machine, the German mathematician Gottfried Wilhelm Leibniz unveiled his 23-year pet project, the Stepped Reckoner. This machine was designed to not only add and subtract, but to multiply, divide and extract square roots. This was a major advance in features, and there was only one thing wrong with the machine — it didn't work.

It did, however, introduce a new concept to "reckoning," and that was "stepping." The concept was to break a mathematical problem into smaller steps, steps so small that the average human would find following that many steps tedious and time-consuming, but steps that a machine could do rather quickly and without noticeable signs of boredom.

Whereas Pascal used ten symbols in each mathematical problem (0, 1, 2, 3, 4, 5, 6, 7, 8, and 9), Leibniz used only two (0 and 1). The former system is called the decimal system (dec meaning ten) and the latter, binary (bi meaning two).

It is far easier for a machine to keep track of only two variables than for it to keep track of ten. Two variables can be represented in very concrete terms — on/off, yes/no, black/white, in/out, up/down, open/closed.

Absolute, concrete terms are something machines like. The gradation of information that humans enjoy machines don't. It is not surprising that a Frenchman devised a gradation machine (0 through 9 in gradual increments) while a German introduced an absolute machine (0 and 1 and that's that). It would later take an Englishman, George Boole, to massage the Teutonic and the Gallic approaches into the system of logic modern computers would eventually use.

• We all know how the decimal system of numbers works — it's the system of counting we use all the time. We have ten symbols (0, 1, 2, 3, 4, 5, 6, 7, 8, and 9). Whenever we use up all the symbols we must start combining symbols to indicate amounts larger than 9. We do this by columns. The right hand column represents the symbol itself. The column to the left of that represents ten times the value of that symbol. The column to the left of that represents ten times ten, or one-hundred times the number. Each column to the left represents an additional ten-fold increase. (Remember, if you start to drift, move on to the next point. None of this is necessary.)

The first four columns of the decimal system are:

THOUSANDS   HUNDREDS   TENS   ONES

To write "eight" one would put an 8 in the ONES column. To write "eighty," or ten times eight, one would write an 8 in the TENS column and a 0 in the ONES column. The long way of reading that would be "Eight TENS and Zero ONES." (Is anyone besides me having flashbacks of second grade?)

The binary system works in the same way, except that there are only two symbols, 0 and 1. As in decimal, the 0 is used to represent nothing. Therefore, after indicating only *one* variable, the binary system needs a new column. The new column, to the left, indicates a number twice as large as the number in the first column. The next column to the left indicates a number twice as large as the preceding column, and so on.

The first four columns of the binary system would be:

EIGHTS   FOURS   TWOS   ONES

"Eight" in binary would have a 1 in the EIGHTS column, a 0 in the FOURS place, a 0 in the TWOS place and a 0 in the ONES place. The long way of reading that would be, "One EIGHT, zero FOURS, zero TWOS, and zero ONES." It would be written 1000. "8" in decimal equals "1000" in binary.

Before we attempt to represent "eighty" in binary, let's first count from zero to ten in binary.

Zero would be 0. One would be 1. So far so good, but

already we've run out of symbols, so we must add a column to the left. Two would be 10 (one TWO and zero ONES). Three would be 11 (one TWO and one ONE). And again we've run out of symbols. We add an additional column and write 100 (one FOUR, zero TWOS and zero ONES). Five is 101 (one FOUR, zero TWOS, and one ONE). Six is 110 (one FOUR, one TWO, and zero ONES). Seven is 111 (one FOUR, one TWO, and one ONE). Again we've run out of symbols, so we add a column, and return to our old friend 1000 (one EIGHT, zero FOURS, zero TWOS, and zero ONES). Nine is 1001 (one EIGHT, zero FOURS, zero TWOS, and one ONE). Ten is 1010 (one EIGHT, zero FOURS, one TWO, and zero ONES).

To get to "eighty" does not require as many columns as one might think, since each time we add a column to

One of the many distinguished scientists who had nothing whatsoever to do with the development of the computer.

the left it doubles the value of the column immediately to its right. The column to the left of EIGHTS would be SIXTEENS, the column to the left of that THIRTY-TWOS, and the column to the left of that SIXTY-FOURS. It seems that extending the columns this far to the left should give us "eighty."

SIXTY-FOURS THIRTY-TWOS SIXTEENS EIGHTS FOURS TWOS ONES

It becomes sort of a puzzle (the sort of a puzzle which I, by the way, dislike) — "Using a maximum of one number from each column, arrive at the number 'eighty.'"

Let's see, a SIXTY-FOUR and a THIRTY-TWO would give us ninety-six. Over the top already. A SIXTY-FOUR and a SIXTEEN equal — ta-da — eighty. (Boy, did we luck out on that one.) So, we would write "eighty" in binary 1010000 (one SIXTY-FOUR, zero THIRTY-TWOS, one SIXTEEN, zero EIGHTS, zero FOURS, zero TWOS, and zero ONES).

(Challenge: Write the number "twenty-seven" in binary numbers.)

It would seem as though one would require reams of paper to record large numbers in binary. Actually, this is not the case. Because the columns continue to double as they move to the left, the binary system becomes increasingly compact. Whereas it takes seven binary columns to write the decimal number 64 (1000000), it takes only forty binary columns to write the decimal number 549,755,813,888 (10000000000000000000000000000000000000000).

Do you need to know any of this to operate a personal computer? No. None of it. It will, however, help answer the question, "Why are there 64K in the memory of my computer?" Because the Kilobyte ratings of computer memories are usually equal to a binary column number (4K, 8K, 16K, 32K, 64K, 128K, 256K, and so on).

Your computer will accept information in standard decimal form and return processed information in standard decimal form. All conversions to and from binary will take place within the computer.

(Answer to the challenge: "twenty-seven" binary is 11011.)

• A computer is very simple minded. It knows only two things: Yes and No. There are no Maybes. A circuit is either open or it's closed. There is no little-bit-open or almost-closed. It's black or white, no grey whatsoever. It's 0 or 1.

There are two reasons why computers can do all that they do knowing as little as they do.

1. SIZE. A great many yes/no circuits can fit into a very small space. As we saw above, it would take only 40 yes/no circuits to write all numbers from one to one trillion. Computer technology is such that you can hold *millions* of these yes/no circuits in the palm of your hand. This miniaturization allows the computing power of room-sized 1950-computers to fit into the pocket calculators of today. These yes/no circuits are so cheap that you can buy for $100 what would have cost you $1,000,000 thirty years ago.

2. SPEED. One of these little yes/no circuits can say "no" faster than Debbie Boone. Properly induced, it can say "yes" just as fast. This is because each circuit is opened or closed electronically, not mechanically. (There are not millions of little fingers turning millions of little switches on and off.) This means that computers compute at speeds approaching one-fourth the speed of light. In fact, most of the time a computer takes to compute something is in interacting with a mechanical device, such as a disk drive or a joystick.

The speed at which computers operate is so incomprehensible that someone devised this comparison: If you were interacting with a computer — you giving the computer data, the computer giving you data, back and forth — it would take you each time, in the computer's time frame, *eight years* to respond. Having to work as they do with binary numbers and human beings, it is fortunate that computers are not easily bored.

• It was the lack of these two elements, size and speed, that prevented Charles Babbage from constructing a fully-functioning personal computer almost 150 years ago.

By 1835 Babbage, an English inventor, had conceived an "Analytical Engine" that incorporated almost every other element of computing, including programming, memory, printout, and the ever-popular punch cards.

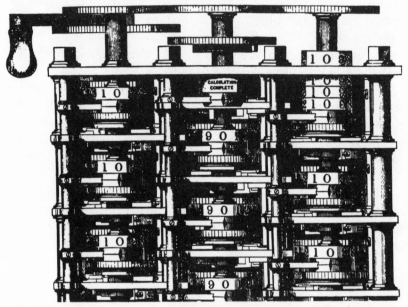

A small portion of Babbage's Analytical Engine.

But Babbage lacked the technology of size and speed, and his 1835 invention of the computer would go unnoticed and forgotten until his writings were rediscovered in 1937.

• Babbage used punch cards borrowed from the Jacquard loom, which Jacquard borrowed from the Vaucanson loom, which Vaucanson borrowed from the Bouchon loom, which Bouchon — the son of an organ maker — borrowed from the automated organ. (This organ to loom to computer connection is delightfully delineated in James Burke's *Connections*, both on the PBS television series and in the Little, Brown and Company book.)

Back in the days of the automated organ (the sixteenth century, give or take a century) a peg was placed on a revolving cylinder for each "yes." As the cylinder turned, the peg would strike a note. This same principle is used in music boxes today.

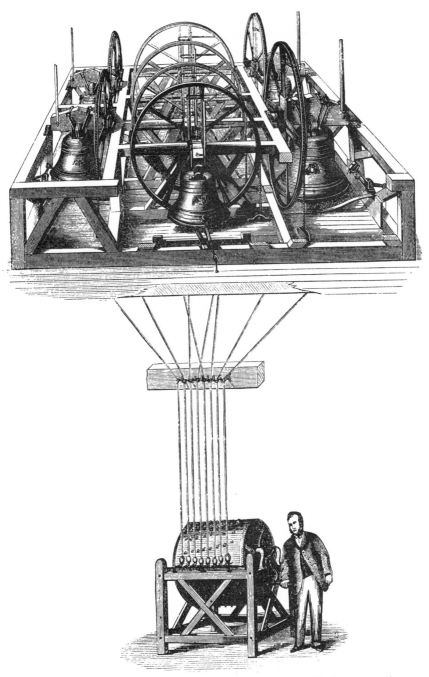

Each time a peg on the drum of this automated bell-ringer pulls a string, the bell attached to that string rings.

The automated weaving looms used paper with holes in it. If a rod could fit in the hole, the thread would be included in the design. If there was no hole for the rod to slip into, the thread would not. This allowed for intricate, inexpensive, and error-free weaving. It's the same concept seen in player piano rolls and computer punch cards.

Punch cards — which until just a few years ago would arrive almost daily in the mail with the ominous warning not to fold, spindle, or mutilate them — work like this:

The card is designed with room to punch out little holes. These holes represent a basic yes/no binary circuit — if the hole is punched, that's yes; if the hole is not punched, that's no. These holes could be assigned to record any answer whatsoever, providing that the answer was either yes or no.

Let's take a very simple punch card that would offer someone the choice of a hot dog, a hamburger, or both. The card would look something like this —

```
┌─────────────────────────────────────────────┐
│                                               │
│          □                      □             │
│                                               │
│      HOT DOG              HAMBURGER           │
│                                               │
└─────────────────────────────────────────────┘
```

If one wanted a hot dog, he or she would punch-out the hole above hot dog and leave the hamburger hole alone. The "Yes, I want a hot dog; no, I do not want a hamburger" card would look like this —

```
┌─────────────────────────────────────────────┐
│                                               │
│          ■                      □             │
│                                               │
│      HOT DOG              HAMBURGER           │
│                                               │
└─────────────────────────────────────────────┘
```

This card would communicate to a computerized kitchen, "I would like a hamburger but not a hot dog":

```
         □                        ■

     HOT DOG                  HAMBURGER
```

This card would say, "I am obviously hungry. I would like a hot dog *and* a hamburger."

```
         ■                        ■

     HOT DOG                  HAMBURGER
```

And an unpunched card might mean, "I am on a diet. Do you have any cottage cheese?"

In this way, a card with only two holes has given us four possible choices — hamburger only, hot dog only, hamburger and hot dog, neither hamburger nor hot dog. The choices given the card puncher could be geometrically increased by simply adding a few more holes.

```
         □                        □

     HOT DOG                  HAMBURGER

   □      □      □      □      □      □      □

 KETCHUP MUSTARD RELISH PICKLE ONION TOMATO CHILI
```

This would offer a range of choices from nothing, to a hamburger *and* a hot dog with everything.

Punch cards, once very popular, have been almost entirely replaced by magnetic disks and tapes. IBM is in the process of recycling billions of these cards. To get some cards for your bird, write IBM, Boca Raton, Florida.

• The 1880 census in the United States took eight years to count. What with the tired and the poor and the huddled masses steaming to America from the teeming shores of Europe, it was estimated that the 1880 census would be counted by 1902. At that rate we would know, by 1985, what the population was in 1930. A better way of counting and sorting was needed and was duly discovered: The 1890 Census Machine.

John Shaw Billings, a medical doctor and lieutenant-colonel in the U.S. Army, came up with the idea of using the punch-hole cards to speed people counting, and turned the project over to Herman Hollerith.

Hollerith designed cards that the census takers could carry with them and punch in the field. The cards included information on sex, age, birth date, nationality — the standard census data. Then the cards were processed by a machine. Each time a hole was in a card, a metal rod would pass through, complete an electrical circuit, and the data was tabulated. However primitive, and although the balance of this computer was purely mechanical, this was the first use of an electric circuit in computing.

The 1890 census was completed, thanks to the computer, in less than three years. In 1911 Hollerith joined with the Computing Tabulating Recording Company, which later became IBM.

• The next two advances came from those hotbeds of progress, war and universities.

By 1939, IBM had become a grand American institution. It joined with another grand American institution, Harvard, and together they made a computer, the Mark I. Partly electrical and partly mechanical, it was the world's largest adding machine. It was fifty feet long and eight feet high. It could add, subtract, multiply, divide, and — most importantly — make mathematical tables. The tables were used by the military in World War II. It told them, for example, where to aim a gun so that the shell and the enemy plane would reach the same place at the same time.

Until WWII, big guns were only asked to fire on stationary objects, like buildings, or on slowly-moving objects, like ships. Airplanes moved at several hundred

The 1890 Census Machine.

miles an hour. The gunner needed to know *exactly* how far in front of the plane to aim. Hence a book of intricate tables was devised that almost required a computer to interpret.

Meanwhile, the University of Pennsylvania, not to be outdone, was working on the first fully electronic computer, the ENIAC (Electronic Numerical Integrator and Calculator). Was this, too, the birth of computer jargon?

The ENIAC took up 3,000 cubic feet (some computer *stores* today are smaller than that), weighed 30 tons, and used 18,000 vacuum tubes. On the average, one tube failed every seven minutes. (When they say that computers today are very reliable, they may be comparing them to the ENIAC.)

The ENIAC was a big hit. When it was first plugged in in 1946 (the year my parents got married — ah, memories) it spent two hours doing nuclear-physics calculations that would have taken 100 engineers one year to compute. How many hours it took ENIAC to come up with *that* statistic we will never know.

Hard at work, designing the first IBM at Harvard.

• Remington Rand introduced the Univac in 1951. It was the first computer that could handle both numbers *and* letters. The computer was taught to read and write. The first customer in line for the Univac were the folks who started it all back in 1890 — the United States Bureau of Census.

• I love full circles. Here are two more.

Magnetic tape — developed by the Germans during WWII while American computers used paper-punch input to devise gun charts — became the standard storage medium for computers during the 1950s. Those are reels of magnetic tape spinning in the science fiction movies of the period.

The Japanese, still happy with their abacuses, took a neglected invention from the Bell Laboratories — the transistor — and revolutionized the world with it. It began with the transistor radio in the late 1950s and moved to computers in the early 1960s.

Each small, cool, inexpensive, reliable transistor replaced a large, hot, expensive, volatile vacuum tube. Computers became smaller, cooler, less expensive, and more reliable.

The inside of a transistor as seen through an electron microscope. (SCALE: 1 inch = 4 miles.)

• The late 1960s saw the development of the silicon chip. Each chip, the size of a postage stamp, held the computing power of thousands of transistors, which had replaced thousands of tubes. The ENIAC's 18,000 vacuum tubes and the 30 tons of wiring necessary to connect all those tubes could now fit on a table top.

• The first personal computer was introduced in 1975. The Altair 8800 was a kit offered to hobbyists. It was remarkably — and surprisingly — successful.

Soon the Apple — named after one of its inventor's summer job in an apple orchard — made its debut. It cost $666.66. The Apple was born with a case of the cutes from which it has yet to recover.

Tandy Radio Shack, combining its hobbyist beginnings and its knowledge of marketing electronics to a mass audience, introduced the TRS (Tandy Radio Shack) 80 Model I.

Commodore, maker of hand-held calculators, took the plunge and introduced the PET.

Then the rest of the world jumped in. Entrepreneurs, corporations, shamen, geniuses, bankers, San Fernando Valley housewives, adding machine companies, photocopy companies, and, finally, IBM, all introduced personal computers or peripherals or programs to a waiting but cautious world.

"The equivalent of 10,000 transistors
in this little thing? Amazing."

To help us better understand how computers operate, consider the mechanical rabbit. Rubber band (B) turns wheel (C) which moves gear (D) and pulls rod (E). That should certainly clarify the operation of personal computers

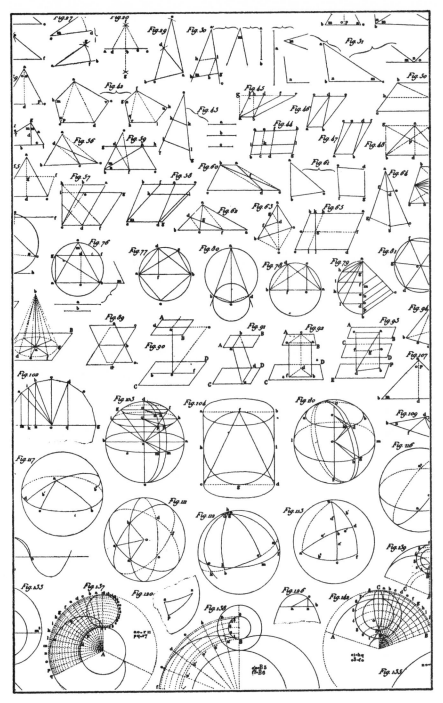

For those who find the "mechanical rabbit" explanation too elementary, here is a more detailed—although equally lucid— diagram

Of Programs and Programming

There is a misconception in the land. The misconception says that, in order to program your computer, you must learn something special, like programming. You don't.

To program a computer, all you need to do is put a disk in a disk drive, or put a cassette in a cassette player, and push a button. That's it. Within a short period of time (several seconds for the disk; several minutes for the cassette) your computer will be programmed.

Here is a program called The WORD. It is available on either 5¼- or 8-inch disks. The program will, within seconds, turn a personal computer into a 45,000-word spell-check dictionary.

A personal computer is like a TV. In order to watch a program on television, all you do is turn it on and set the dial. To change programs, all you do is turn the dial or, more frequently these days, push a button. If none of the programs offered by the stations appeal to you, you can program the TV yourself by playing a video tape or a video disk.

It's precisely the same with a computer. The difference is that, more often than not, you'll start by playing a tape or a disk. (In the world of personal computers one does not *play* a program, one **runs** a program. You would *run* a checkbook program or *run* a word processing program.)

Pardon me for over-making this point, but you have no idea how many people are terrified by personal computers because they've heard how much trouble it is to "program the thing." Programming the thing is as easy as programming your cassette player to play a Beethoven sonata. Running a program is as easy as playing a tape.

There is a great difference, however, between *running* a program and *writing* a program, and therein the confusion lies.

Writing a program for a computer takes a lot of work. First you must learn a computer language. Like any alien, computers have their own languages. These are the ones you may have heard bandied about in computer magazines — BASIC, Fortran, Pascal, Assembly, and so on. Although these languages are not as difficult to learn as, say, Latin, they are far more difficult than pig-Latin.

Second, computers are precise and exacting. If, in a long program of thousands and thousands of lines, there is *one* character out of place, chances are the computer will not run the program properly.

Third, since writing a computer program is, like any other writing, a creative act, one never knows quite how it's going to turn out until the product is finished. It might not, in other words, work. Or it might work in some parts but not in others. Or it might work the first five times but not the sixth. Or....the variety of ways in which a program *won't* work is infinite.

5 Aethiopisch.

7 Zend.

6 Syrisch

3ᵇ Tibetisch.

Some computer languages.

The causes of these irritating and often unpredictable program failures are many and varied, but they all fall under the general classification of **bugs**. The painstaking process of removing bugs is known as **debugging**. Trying to get all the bugs out of some programs is like trying to get all the bugs out of a picnic.

It is little wonder, then, that writing programs has a generally negative reputation among ordinary humans, rather like the reputation the Polar Bear Clubs have. I cringe when I even *think* about the news footage of those people, in bathing suits, cutting holes in the ice and jumping in. *Voluntarily.* I likewise cringe when I see a program printed in a computer magazine — page after page after page of numbers, jargon, and meaningless symbols. The thought of having to copy — much less write — all of that nonsense is enough to put a person off computers permanently. (Alas, in too many cases, I fear it already has.)

This is further complicated by the choice of words those who write programs use. Generally, they don't say, "I had such trouble writing a program last night." Instead, they say, "I had such trouble *programming my computer* last night." (Emphasis mine.) This is like a Polar Bear Club member casually mentioning that he or she "went for a swim." In February. In Vermont.

It should be pointed out that some people *like* jumping in cold water, and some people *like* writing computer programs — and some people like heated swimming pools and pre-written, pre-tested programs. I don't think you'll have much trouble guessing which category I fall into.

Writing a program for a computer is the same as making your own program for television. It can be done and it can be fun, but if you're like most people, the majority of what you watch on television was made by others, and the majority of what you run on your computer will be written by others.

There was a time — only six or seven years ago — when there were no prepackaged, commercially available computer programs. This was because there were so few personal computers. (The first one, you'll remember, was introduced in 1975.) Besides, at that time small computers were in the hands of the hobbyists, and programming the computer was *part* of the process. Back then you might just as well have asked someone to come in and do the soldering on your Heathkit as buy a prewritten computer program.

This corresponds to the early days of recorded sound. After Edison invented (almost by accident) the phonograph, the only practical use he could conceive for the device was as a dictating machine. For the first decade or so, the average library featured more homemade recordings than store-bought. "Grandma Parkins on her 80th birthday." "Uncle Seth sings 'Oh Susanna.' " "Reverend Thompson readin' from the Holy Writ."

John Philip Sousa and Caruso did for the phonograph what Milton Berle and Sid Caesar did for television or Visi-Calc did for personal computers. People wanted the *program* so much that they were willing to buy whatever machine was necessary to play the program on. (The machines — phonographs, TVs, computers — are known as **hardware** and the programs — tapes, videodisks, records — are known as **software**.)

VisiCalc is a program that allows one to enter column after column of interrelated information — an electronic version of the spreadsheets businesspersons have been using for years. The difference with VisiCalc is that, when a change in one figure in one column is made, all the other figures in all the other columns change accordingly, automatically, instantly.

Now this may not mean much to ordinary folk, but to businesspeople this was a breakthrough in trade on a level with, say, opening the Suez Canal. Hours of figuring cost projections eliminated. Days of waiting for revised estimates reduced to seconds. The all-important "bottom line" was never more instantly reached, and the hundreds of components that resulted in the bottom line were never more manageable.

VisiCalc was designed to run on the Apple II Computer. The whole package — VisiCalc, Apple, and video screen — ran around $2,500. *Never mind* $2,300 of that was for the Apple and the video screen and $200 for the VisiCalc. Businesspeople wanted VisiCalc, and if they had to buy an Apple to go with it, so be it.

VisiCalc has become the best selling computer program of all time. It in no small way contributed to Apple's success. Soon, of course, every computer had its version of an electronic spreadsheet program. There are now dozens available, all lumped under the general category of VisiClones.

Another advance in the marketing of programs was **CP/M**. CP/M stands for Control Program for Microprocessors. It is a program that tells the computer how to retrieve and store information on disks. Prior to CP/M, there were several different systems for storing information — all incompatible. (Apple, Radio Shack, IBM, and Commodore still use incompatible formats.) CP/M allowed the smaller computer manufacturer to offer a machine with a standardized disk operating system. If a machine was "CP/M compatible," it could run almost any program written in the CP/M format.

With thousands of Apples (and Radio Shacks and CP/M-based computers) in the field, it became profitable for companies to market software — and so they have. Today there are thousands of prewritten programs, covering a wide range of subjects, from games to business to ecology.

We'll discuss some of these in the chapters that follow, although a full review of all available programs is far beyond the scope of this book.

<hr>

There is a difference, however, between running a computer program and watching a television program. Computer programs generally require some interaction, whereas television programs will go on and on, totally oblivious to what you are or are not doing.

Learning to interact with a computer program, like learning how to use any tool, can take from one minute to several months. Computer programs, are tools. They will help you get your work done with less effort and in less time. Like tools, computer programs come in varying degrees of complexity. Some tools, like the hammer, can be learned within a few minutes. Other tools — the lathe, for example — would take longer. And so it is with computer programs. Space Invaders might take two minutes to learn, an accounting program several weeks. But, like tools, once learned, they may take years to master.

Programs that are easy to learn are called **user friendly**. I'm not sure what programs that are not easy to learn are called, but I've run into a few user unfriendly ones, and a couple that have been downright hostile. One must be careful, however, that the friendliness does not become a burden after one learns the program. The training wheels on a bicycle are helpful but, if not eventually removed, may prove cumbersome.

Learning to operate a new program will require time. Even if you already know how to drive, learning the locations of the various knobs and dipsticks on a new car will take some study and patience. If you've never driven (i.e., operated a computer) before, the investment of time and patience will be greater.

Programming a computer is effortless, learning how to use that program will require some time and study, but you will never, ever — unless you really want to — have to write that program yourself.

"You know, Santa, if I had a personal computer and a modem, we could handle next year's gift list with a great deal more efficiency."

Data Banks

Data banks are like money banks. Money banks gather, store, and distribute money; data banks gather, store, and distribute data.

Data are (yes, "data" is a plural, the singular being "datum," although the use of "data" as a singular is becoming more widely used) anything that goes into a computer, everything stored in a computer's memory, and anything that comes out. "Data" is a general word, like "writing," that covers a broad spectrum of information.

A personal computer can store a limited amount of data — limited in not only amount, but also timeliness. Larger computers (known as **mainframe** computers) can hold almost unlimited amounts of information, and the operators of large computers can afford to have that information constantly updated.

One could not buy a program that would give up-to-the-minute stock market information. One could not buy a program that told the ongoing happenings in, say, Pakistan. One could not buy a program that gave the current price of gold, or the temperature in Tokyo, or which market in town had the lowest price on canned orange juice.

You could, however, rent time on a larger computer that *could* tell you all that — and a great deal more.

There are companies whose business it is to maintain massive amounts of information on a vast variety of subjects, and to rent access to that information by the hour.

The three largest data bank companies are CompuServe, The Source, and The Dow Jones Information Service. CompuServe and The Source offer a potpourri of information, while The Dow Jones Information Service, as you may have guessed, specializes in business — and especially stock market — news. (The Dow Jones company publishes *The Wall Street Journal* and is the instigator of the famous Dow Jones stock market averages — "The Dow Jones Industrials are up one-half point in heavy trading.")

To use the services of one of these data banks is

relatively easy. First, you'll need a modem so that your computer can send and receive information (data) over regular telephone lines. Some personal computers require, too, that you run special "communications software" whenever you use a modem.

Then you dial the local telephone number (or the toll-free WATS number) of the service you want, and enter your identification number and password (given to you when you subscribe to the service). That's all there is to it — you are then "on line" with the world, or at least as much of the world as a given data bank is willing to offer.

Let's take a closer look at the three most popular data banks.

The Source is owned by *Reader's Digest*, "From condensing articles to expanding the limits of personal computing, *The Reader's Digest* is serving *you*."

To subscribe to The Source, one must fill out an application and pay $100. "Can't I just give you my Visa card number over the phone, and you give me an account number and a password?" I asked when I called to subscribe.

"Oh, no," the woman at the other end responded, almost shocked by the impropriety of my question. "We must have a signed form on file before you can use The Source." She articulated the words "signed form" particularly well, as though she were talking to someone who was not very good at understanding English.

A bit more than a month later my unsigned form arrived in the mail. I signed the form, returned it, and two weeks later a notebook arrived UPS.

The notebook was a standard three-ring binder with elaborately printed pages telling everything The Source had to offer — and a few things The Source did not have to offer.

It seems the *New York Times* had removed their data bank from The Source because the *New York Times* rented their data bank at more than $100 per hour and The Source was renting it for less than $25. This was fine as long as The Source specialized in those "toy" home computers but, as personal computers grew more sophisticated and widely used, the *NYT* found that more and more people were dropping the $100-plus service and getting the same information from The Source for under $25. The *Times* dropped The Source.

Dropped by The Source was a rather interesting plan called Legis-Slate that would have allowed one to track any piece of legislation through any state or federal legislative body. It sounds like an ambitious project, and it was — a bit too ambitious.

The Source still has a great deal to offer, including the news of United Press International, detailed stock market reporting, and a vast assortment of programs and information services for both home and business.

After some fiddling (data bases require that one use a **dumb terminal**, or its equivalent — and some smart computers struggle against ever becoming dumb again), I entered my ID number, then my password (if "GNLQFC" qualifies as a word), and I was "On line with The Source."

I was welcomed to The Source and urged to check the monthly discount specials offered by Comp-U-Star, The Source's at-home shopping service. I was then presented with The Entry Screen.

The entry screen gives one the choice of having an overview of The Source, instructions on how to use The Source, being shown The Source Main Menu, or going directly into the Command Level.

A menu in computing, like a menu in a restaurant, lists all that's available. The command level lets one bypass the menu and go directly into a program, rather like saying to the waiter, "Skip the menu and bring us two cheese-burgers."

The Main Menu on The Source looks something like this:

1. News and Reference Resources
2. Business/Financial Markets
3. Catalog Shopping
4. Home and Leisure
5. Education and Career
6. Mail and Communications
7. Creating and Computing
8. Source*Plus

These are the general headings under which hundreds of other choices are listed. If one were to choose "Home and Leisure," for example, the secondary menu would read:

1. Games
2. Advice & Horoscopes
3. Travel & Dining
4. Entertainment
5. Home Finance

Each of these choices would have an additional menu, and so it would go until, by a process of refinement, one would arrive at the information or program one wanted.

From the main menu I chose #6, "Mail and Communications." The Mail and Communications sub-menu was:

1. Mail
2. Chat
3. Post

Simple, direct — and I knew nothing more about The Source's "Mail and Communications" services than I did before. I pushed "1" for Mail. I was told, by yet another menu, that I could check my mail, or send mail to someone else. I love mail, so I thought I would check my mail. This being my first ten minutes on The Source, naturally, there was no mail. "You have to send a letter to get a letter," as my mother used to say. Still, I thought there might have been a welcome note from someone at The Source, something akin to the free box of chocolates you get when you check into the Ritz Carlton in Chicago.

But, no, there was no mail. Did I want to send a letter? I had my choice of anyone on The Source. The trouble was I didn't *know* anyone on The Source. For a moment I considered sending a letter to myself, but then I thought that the computer at The Source might think me pathetic, so I decided not to.

I went on to #2, "Chat." Chat allows one to have a video-to-video discussion with anyone who happens to be on-line with The Source at that time. Again, not knowing anyone on The Source severely limited my use of this feature. (I later discovered that, by using Directory, one can find out the ID numbers of everyone on-line who has an interest in, say, photography. You can also list yourself and interests in the Directory and who knows? Maybe someone will call and Chat with you.)

I moved along to #3, "Post." Post is sort of an electronic classified ad section. One can post a message in any of 75 categories, such as art, antiques, automobiles, and so on. I went right to "dating." I was told there were 27 entries. They were rather mild, compared with some "dating" classifieds I've read, but not bad considering the source of The Source is *The Reader's Digest*. "Ever made it with a programmer?" one asks. "Two women want to meet straight men in San Francisco," reads another. (Good luck.)

In addition to the general classification, each ad has a "Subject" entered by the person placing the ad. One need not read the entire ad if the subject does not appeal. (The Source's version of a plain, unmarked envelope?) One subject line was "1 YEAR OLD GIRL WANTED!" Prurient interest or no, I had to read that ad. It was, as expected, placed by a fairly young, fairly inexperienced typist. The ad itself read, "IF ANY GIRL OUT THERE IS 14 AND LIKES GUYS PLEASE CONTACT ME."

Another young man entered the following classified at 12:07 AM: "IF YOU ARE LOOKING FOR A CHARMING 17 YEAR OLD DO NOT HESITATE TO GET IN TOUCH WITH ME." He either thought his message could stand a bit of clarification, or was it just the impatience of youth?, because at 12:16 AM he was back with another ad, "IF YOU ARE LOOKING FOR AN ATTRACTIVE 17 YEAR OLD MALE THEN GET IN TOUCH WITH ME." Androgynous charm or masculine straightforwardness, one has one's choice.

I do not mean to imply that The Source is merely a video version of a singles' bar (although they do feature extensive information on wine). No, there's Jack Anderson, too. And weather, sports, dining guides, movie reviews, commodity prices, and on and on and on.

I recommend calling The Source directly (toll free 800-336-3330) and asking for their current catalog of rates and services. If you are not happy with The Source within the first 30 days, the $100 registration fee is refundable, less charges for actual on-line time. If you are not happy with The Source any time after 30 days, you can register a public (public to all other Source subscribers) complaint on a bulletin board known as "Gripes."

The computers used at data banks have large disk drives that permit almost unlimited storage.

More liberal than The Source with their initial sign-on policy is CompuServe. All it takes is going into your local Radio Shack store and plunking down $19.95. You can't get more liberal than that. Finding a Radio Shack store that *has* the dumb terminal package (the package for computers other than Radio Shack Computers) is another matter. One.Radio Shack Computer Center — in Beverly Hills no less — didn't have it. "When will you get one in?" "Oh, in two to four weeks."

I decided to let my fingers do the walking to the other Radio Shack Computer Centers, and found one that had the Dumb Terminal Package. I talked to a salesman — let's call him Ollie — and asked him to hold one dumb terminal package for me.

When I arrived at the store, Ollie was especially happy to see me. Were things that tough that the commission on a $19.95 sale would cause such friendliness? He said he was holding the dumb terminal package for me and would be right out with it.

Moments later Ollie wheeled out a box the size of a small dishwasher. "Here's your dumb terminal package," he announced proudly.

Now, I was an assistant manager of a Radio Shack store in my younger, more desperate days, and I knew that Radio Shack wouldn't sell the *box*, much less the contents of a box that large, for $19.95. What he was trying to sell me was a dumb terminal. "No, I want the package for CompuServe," I explained.

"Yes," Ollie said, still counting his commission, "This gets CompuServe. This gets Dow Jones (I am convinced he thought Dow Jones was a TV program like *Barney Miller*). This gets everything." Before he could tell me about the Radio Free Europe option, I explained that I already *had* a terminal, and all I wanted was an ID number and a password.

Another salesman, thankfully, overheard my comments. He pulled a notebook off a shelf and showed Ollie what I was looking for. There was joy as understanding dawned in Ollie's eyes, followed by disappointment as he realized his commission would not be as great as he had hoped.

While Ollie calculated the sales tax (and his commission) on $19.95, I opened the package and read a little. It was a standard Radio Shack software folder they must produce by the millions. It had a three-ring binder with two slim booklets in it, one describing CompuServe, the other describing The Dow Jones Information Service. The inside front cover had eight cassette tape pockets standing empty. (Radio Shack still markets a great many programs on cassettes.)

A sealed packet contained my ID number and password. I knew this because the packet clearly stated: "For security reasons your User Identification Number and Secret Password should be kept separate. Memorize your Secret Password, then keep it in a safe place." One's brain is not a safe place, I take it.

The packet also said, "Obtain the local network telephone number for your area at the point of purchase." Ollie asked for $21.24, so I assumed that this was my point of purchase. I showed Ollie the sentence. He read it and gave me a number. I wrote it on the packet. I apologized for the mix-up, took my change, and went home.

The basic CompuServe package includes one hour on both CompuServe and the Dow Jones Information Service. These hours must be non-prime time — after 6 PM for CompuServe and after 8 PM for Dow Jones, anytime weekends and holidays.

Somewhere around seven that evening I put my computer into the dumb terminal mode (after doing it once for The Source it was easy) and called the "local network telephone number." Ollie answered. He had given me his phone number.

"Ollie," I said, "Do you have the number for CompuServe?"

"Oh, yes," he said, and rattled off another phone number. With minor trepidation I dialed the number. Would it be his sister? Another phone in his house? A deli? New Delhi? One thing was certain: it was not going to be CompuServe. It wasn't. It was the Radio Shack Computer Center.

Not prepared for an elaborate explanation, I blurted

out, "What's CompuServe's number?" The salesperson gave me a phone number, I checked to make sure it wasn't Ollie's, and dialed it. I got the welcome, high pitched noise that means "The computer on this end of the line is ready. Turn on your modem." I did, and was on-line with Compu-Serve in a matter of minutes.

(If you have trouble getting connected with or operating The Source, they supply a toll-free number. CompuServe had no such number.)

The CompuServe main menu was:

1. Newspapers
2. Finance
3. Entertainment
4. Communications
5. CompuServe User Information
6. Special Services
7. Home Information

9. MicroNET Personal Computing

What the phantom "8" once represented is never told. Did the *New York Times* pull out of CompuServe, too? Could there have been a run on the data banks?

Although it covers the same basic territory as The Source, CompuServe appears to be a marginally lighter-weight information service. Still, it's fun, and certainly worth $19.95 for a trial hour of poking about its programs and services. (A booklet on CompuServe's offerings is available from Radio Shack, Fort Worth, Texas, 76102.)

The Dow Jones Information Service, on the other hand, is heavyweight all the way, and I mean heavy in the heaviest sense of the word. This is big time, big business, and it's very serious. No *Off The Wall Street Journal* here.

The Wall Street Journal is represented, as are *Barrons*, the *Dow Jones News Service* (known around the Big Board as the Broadtape), and transcripts of the television show *Wall Street Week*.

Also available are stock market quotations (delayed 15 minutes, as they are on all services), plus in-depth financial reports on all New York and American Stock Exchange companies and 800 selected over-the-counter companies.

The Dow Jones Information Service has a toll-free customer assistance number, but its hours do not include late-night nor Sundays. They are reachable at 800-257-5114.

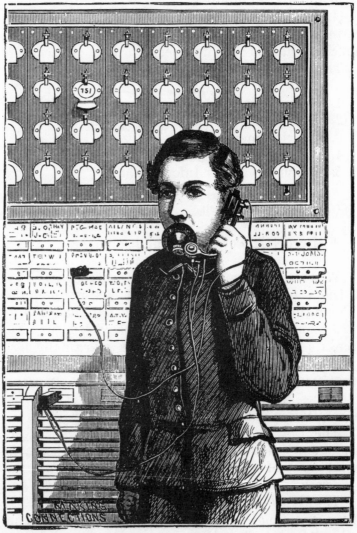

"Hello. Dow Jones Information Service. Computer Room. Tim speaking. Oh, hello, Mr. President. No, there's been no sign of an upswing in the economy in the last 45 minutes. Yes, sir. We'll call you just as soon as it happens. Thank you, sir. Goodbye."

Between programs you buy and run, and data banks which you rent by the hour, the personal computer becomes a powerful tool, one that is capable of doing all the things for home, business, and education we're about to explore.

"If I had a computer,
I'd com-pute in the morning,
I'd com-pute in the evening,
All over this land . . ."

"You promise me a computer and what do I get? Nothing.
Get off the cat. Nothing. That's what I get."

The Uses of
Personal Computers

"Come on up. I'll show you my Atari."

Personal computers are just that — personal. People buy — or do not buy — personal computers for the same sensible or capricious reasons that they, say, get married, or move to New York, or buy a new car.

For some people, the fact that a computer can do just one thing is enough. Young people fall in love with a specific video game with the same passion that previous generations pined away for little red wagons or model trains. If having 24-hour access to that game means owning a computer, so be it. Businesspeople might find the ability to send and receive electronic mail more than worth a personal computer's cost. The fact that a personal computer can process words ten times more efficiently than even the best electronic typewriters is all that many writers need to know.

Yet, for most people, the decision to buy or not to buy a personal computer is less clear cut. Yes, it would be *nice* to have a machine that does this and this and this, but is it worth $5,000, or $3,000, or even $99.95? And if money is not an object, then time is. Is it worth the time it will take to learn how to use this new gadget? That espresso machine from Christmas, 1979, is still sitting in the kitchen cupboard, and it has yet to make a single cup of coffee.

For most people, the decision to buy a personal computer is a process of crystallization. When a crystal is formed, say an ice crystal, the temperature of the water falls and falls, the molecules move slower and slower, yet it remains water. Then, suddenly, around 32° F — or 0° C, for you metric fans — the liquid turns to solid and a crystal is formed. The water does not become harder and harder, like drying wax, until it's eventually solid. One moment it's a liquid, the next moment it's a solid. The water has crystallized.

I have observed people, while deciding to buy or not to buy a personal computer, go through the same process. You hear about personal computers for the first time —

Taken from "The Personal Computer Book."

some mention of corruption in Silicon Valley on *Sixty Minutes* — but the water temperature remains a balmy 72°. (Since we have, as a nation, officially abandoned metric, all temperatures given will be in Fahrenheit.)

Then you hear about computer games, electronic mail, discount shopping. The water falls to a nippy 53°. Then someone actually *demonstrates* word processing, accounting, electronic spreadsheeting. The temperature dips to 39°.

Then a friend says how much fun he had "chatting" with a stranger in Oregon. Another friend said she made an airline reservation without having to be put on hold and listen to Muzak courtesy of the Friendly Skies. Yet another friend tells how he lost at chess, but he lost to a computer program that beat Bobby Fischer. The water drops to 34°, and the Polar Bear Club Members arrive en masse.

Finally your grandmother calls and says that she stayed up until 3 AM playing Ms. Pac-Man. That does it. The temperature falls to 31°. The crystal has formed. Your next major life project: Get a computer.

The uses of personal computers have been arbitrarily divided into several chapters, exploring the benefits of personal computers in the home, in business, in education, word processing, and games. This is an overlapping group of headings. Certainly word processing could take place in business, in the home, and in education. Games, too, could fit into the same three categories. Education — especially with personal computers — need not be limited to schools; there's lots to learn and teach in the home and in business.

Above all, please do not use this section as the definitive guide to what personal computers can and cannot do. Even as I write it, it is obsolete. Each day, dozens of new programs are introduced. Each week, several new features are offered on data banks. Each month, a new peripheral or a new personal computer expands the dimensions of personal computing.

Please view this section, then, as an introductory overview. In a few years, this part of the book will appear as silly as the middle section of the 1950 edition of *The TV Book* as it attempted to describe the 1949 television season.

As programs and data banks continue to grow, so does the appeal and usefulness of personal computers.

"Frankincense is very nice, but I was sort of hoping for an Atari."

An early tabulating computer.

Personal Computers in Business

Immediately following the triumphant success of The 1890 Census Machine, the first place computers went, naturally, was business. The company Herman Hollerith, inventor of the 1890 Census Machine, joined did not eventually call itself International *Business* Machines for nothing.

The computers of the early 1900s were nothing more than tabulating machines, and there was little need for tabulation in the home. The 'rithmetic third of the three Rs was more than enough to handle domestic calculating needs.

Besides, even if uses for a computer in the home *were* found, the consumer market was glutted by far less expensive — and far more useful — inventions. The telephone, gramophone, electric light, automobile, washing machine, gas stove, and radio — not to mention indoor plumbing and central heating — were of more interest to the average householder than a faster way to count.

The **FIRST FLUSH**

Taken from "The Personal Computer Book."

Business did have a use for the computer, but it did not adopt the new machine all at once. In the first place, computers didn't do that much. One would have to have needs as specific as the U.S. Census Bureau's to require a computer. In the second place, labor was cheap. Why pay vast amounts of money for a machine to add, subtract, and count when qualified bookkeepers could be had for twenty cents an hour?

As the years went on, however, the computer's capabilities rose — as did the minimum wage — and by the time IBM joined the hallowed ranks of the Fortune 500, one would be hard pressed to not find at least *one* large computer in each of the other 499 companies.

When the personal computer arrived on the scene in the middle of the 1970s, computers were an accepted part of Big Business. The idea that a computer cost hundreds of thousands of dollars and that it had to be programmed at a cost of many thousands more, was so ingrained in the psyche of Big Business that personal computers, costing less than $5,000 — and a pre-written program costing less than $500 — were, for the most part, ignored.

But soon, inroads were made. By the late 1970s there were three types of computers: mainframe computers, costing from $20,000 on into infinity; minicomputers, costing from $5,000 to $20,000; and microcomputers, costing less than $5,000. For a while (a time span that seemed like decades but lasted only a couple of years), the formula was set: If you were a big business you bought a mainframe, if you were a small business you bought a mini, and *nobody* in business bought a micro. To buy a microcomputer for a company was like buying a manual typewriter — no one who was serious about business would even consider it.

VisiCalc, the electronic spreadsheet program mentioned in Chapter Three, changed all that. It was acceptable to buy a microcomputer — usually an Apple — because it performed a necessary financial function that no other office machine could duplicate. The only rule was that the micro be treated with the respect due any other office machine, and not with the respect due a Computer. One could speak fondly of one's Selectric or Xerox or Apple, but one must never hold one's micro in the same reverent light as one would hold The Mainframe.

As programs developed, the businesspersons found that their micros could do far more than electronic spread-sheeting and games. By the time micros stopped being called micros and started being called personal computers, a small computer was an accepted — and invaluable — part of all business, large and small. The final nod of acceptability was given when IBM — *the* IBM — introduced a personal computer of its own.

In the corridors of big business, however, personal computers are not known as personal computers. *Nothing* is personally owned at AT&T. Neither are they known as individual computers, as individuality is not stressed among the ranks of the fortunate 500. In these halls of commerce, personal computers are known as **desktop** computers. IBM is helping to change that, too, by calling their desktop computer The IBM Personal Computer. It's a ·confusing world, nomenclature.

The most obvious beneficiary of the personal computer is the small businessperson. Finally, the benefits (and, alas, headaches) of the computer age are available to even the smallest of small businesses.

A single personal computer can handle accounting, inventory control, word processing, financial projections, and so much more. For the past thirty years these have been the domain of the large computer in the large company, and the cause of endless paperwork in the small company. (Payroll, for a small company, is still best handled by one's bank.)

As it did in big business, a computer can save a small business large amounts of money, while simulta-neously increasing productivity.

A gradually-expanding one-person company might find a personal computer would delay the hiring of a second person for some time. Word processing speeds corres-pondence and accounting eases billing such that a one-person company can remain a one-person company through a doubling or even a tripling of business.

A two-person company (The Boss and The Secretary) might never need to become a three-person company. The Secretary can process so much more information with a personal computer — providing he or she can pry The Boss away from stock market analysis or Missile Command — that the need to become a three-person company might be indefinitely postponed. The Boss might even want to get a personal computer for him or herself.

A three-person company (The Boss, The Secretary, and The Bookkeeper) would find one computer a help, two computers a blessing, and three computers a luxury. The Secretary could do word processing, The Bookkeeper accounting, and The Boss could keep an eye on the commodities market without disturbing the flow of either correspondence or receivables.

In the small companies noted, each personal computer will roughly double the output of The Secretary and The Bookkeeper. The Boss, due to the intrinsic nature of bossdom, could find his or her productivity increased ten fold — or may find the personal computer just an expensive toy. Given that The Boss's productivity remains the same, a personal computer could allow two persons to do the work of three, and three to do the work of five.

After three, however, one reaches a point of diminishing returns. As companies grow, it is necessary to add personnel who are not aided by the addition of a personal computer. Maintenance, messengers, envelope stuffers, warehousing, and similar physical activities are not within the domain of a personal computer's enhanced efficiency.

A salesperson would find that the primary benefit wrought by personal computers is their ability to churn out masses of personalized letters. This would no doubt increase sales, but a salesperson would still spend most of the time on the phone or on the road.

For The Secretary and for The Bookkeeper, almost without exception, the personal computer would be a Godsend.

A Course in Practical Salesmanship
Tuition FREE~All Expenses Paid

IN these times of keen business rivalry, the services of the Trained Salesman command a high premium.

The Oliver Sales Organization is the finest body of Trained Salesmen in the world. It is composed of picked men, and is under the guidance of Sales Experts.

In less than ten years it has placed the Oliver Typewriter where it belongs—in a position of absolute leadership.

Its aggregate earnings are enormous and the individual average is high.

The scope of its activities is as wide as civilization and the greatest prizes of the commercial world are open to its membership.

The organization is drilled like an army. It affords a liberal education in actual salesmanship, and increases individual earning power many per cent, by systematic development of natural talents.

Its ranks are recruited from every walk of life. Men who had missed their calling and made dismal failures in the over-crowded professions have been developed in the Oliver School of Practical Salesmanship into phenomenal successes.

The Oliver Typewriter puts the salesman in touch with the men worth knowing—the human dynamos who furnish the brain power of the commercial world.

Because every Business Executive is interested in the very things the Oliver stands for—economy of time and money—increase in efficiency of Correspondence and Accounting Departments.

The OLIVER Typewriter
The Standard Visible Writer

is simple in principle, compactly built, durable in construction, and its touch is beautifully elastic and most responsive.

In versatility, legibility, perfect alignment, visibility, etc., it is all that could be desired in a writing machine.

It's a constant source of inspiration to the salesman, as every day develops new evidence of its wide range of usefulness.

Just as the winning personality of a human being attracts and holds friends, so does the Oliver, by its responsiveness to all demands, gain and hold an ever-widening circle of enthusiastic admirers.

If you wish to learn actual salesmanship and become a member of the Oliver Organization, send in your application **immediately,** as the ranks are rapidly being filled.

You can take up this work in spare time, or give us your entire time, just as you prefer.

Whether you earn $300 a year, or **twelve times** $300 a year, depends entirely upon **yourself.**

We offer to properly qualified applicants the opportunity to earn handsome salaries and to gain a knowledge of salesmanship that will prove of inestimable value.

Can you afford to vegetate in a poorly-paid position, when the way is open to a successful business career?

Address at once.

THE OLIVER TYPEWRITER CO., 161 Wabash Ave., Chicago

WE WANT LOCAL AGENTS IN THE UNITED STATES AND CANADA.
PRINCIPAL FOREIGN OFFICE—75 QUEEN VICTORIA ST., LONDON.

[1906]

For now, let's see what favours personal computers offer the typical small business bookkeeper. At the same time we'll look at the fears office workers have of computers, where they come from, and how to eliminate them.

The language of accountancy is numbers. Objects the size of locomotives are reduced to model numbers and inventory figures. Everything is broken into its smallest components, and each component has a part number. Pieces of paper are referred to by check number, invoice number, and purchase order number. Each transaction has a transaction number, each service a service number, and each employee an employee number. To a bookkeeper, God is the ultimate accountant, because it is said that He has numbered even the last hair on our heads.

Computers, like bookkeepers, take particularly well to numbers. All the figuring, copying, and keeping accurate track of ciphers is what computers were created to do, and they do it magnificently. They do it so well, in fact, that the superior speed and ability computers have over humans in this area has given rise to the various boogie-man-computer-taking-over-the-world scenarios.

And it is this very fear of "taking over" that can keep a personal computer at the door of an accounting department, longing to get in. The bookkeeper may fear that, once he or she has taught this "thing" everything about the financial workings of the company, the position of bookkeeper will be replaced by a four-dollar-an-hour typist.

Nothing could be further from the truth, and if you are an employer looking to cut costs by *replacing* your bookkeeper with a personal computer, you might as well abandon that idea right now. A company needs someone — a human being someone — to keep track in a numerical way of the ebb and flow of products, materials, people, time, and, of course, money. A computer cannot do this, but a computer can *assist* a human in doing this by removing the miasma of repetitive detail that prevents the human from seeing the larger picture.

In a small company, it is important that the person operating the "accounting computer" has a firm grasp of standard accounting procedures, as well as a knowledge of how company money came and went before the computer came along. The personal computer is an efficient tool in bookkeeping, just as are pencil and paper and general ledger books and electronic calculators. Tools require humans to work them and, the more skilled the worker, the finer the end result.

Another fear many people have is the fear of the unknown, and computers, more than anything, represent "the unknown." Paper is knowable. You can touch it, feel it, write on it, read from it, stack it, file it, fold it, spindle it, mutilate it, and throw it away when you're done with it. But a magnetic disk? A piece of plastic or aluminum covered with rust? "*This* holds the equivalent of fifty general ledger pages? And *this* holds the entire customer file, complete with credit ratings and records of orders and payments for the past five years? And *this* holds the entire inventory, with cost-per-piece, supplier, and year-to-date sales for each item? I want nothing to do with it."

More mysterious is what goes on *inside* the computer, in those dark places where the sacred one-through-nine are transformed into zero-and-one; where precious digits go through the rather violent-sounding ritual of "number crunching."

Fear of computers is very real. It even has a name, cyberphobia — from the word cybernate, meaning to control or become controlled *by* (evil, evil) a computer. This fear affects, according to some estimates, as much as thirty percent of the population. Those thirty percent would never dream of reading this book, any more than people with an even more widespread fear would ever consider reading **The Spider Book**.

An illustration from "The Spider Book."

At work, however, if the boss brings in his or her pet tarantula — or his or her pet computerization project — the employee has three choices: find a new job, find a way to conquer the fear, or find a way to kill the thing. One never knows how a cyberphobic employee will respond, and it is a wise and compassionate employer who has a gradual plan for introducing personal computers into the mainstream of company life.

Here are some suggestions on easing computers into the workplace.

1. Start by dropping subtle hints. In the middle of a task that a worker finds particulaly dull and time-consuming, casually mention, "If we only had a computer, we could get this done in ten minutes." Computers can and do eliminate dozens of boring and repetitive office procedures, and the thought that one never again had to alphabetize the mailing list or add an endless column of numbers might spark some curiosity about this awful machine.

2. For every task you point out that a computer can do, point out three that it cannot. Whenever an employee performs a task that required ingenuity, intelligence, wit — or even hands — be sure to say, "We'll never replace *you* with a computer!" Be sure to stress the "you." This is known as positive reinforcement. It is important to get across the point that personal computers in small businesses do not replace people, they help people do their jobs easier, faster, and better.

"We'll never replace you with a computer."

3. Talk to people about the *idea* of getting a computer. Do not announce one day, "You're getting a computer — what kind do you want?" To some people that's like announcing, "We're moving to Afghanistan — how do you want to get there, by boat or by plane?" Start slowly with the concept, and build from there.

4. Discuss *programs* rather than *computers*. Computers are, to most people, fairly uninteresting machines. It's the *programs* that do the work, and in that lies the fascination. Point out what a spell-check program or an electronic spreadsheet program or an accounts receivable program might do and how it works.

For example, the PeachTree Software Company has Invoicing and Inventory programs that tie into their Series 8 Accounts Receivable program. These programs have speeded up the processing of invoices by several magnitudes around Prelude Press.

The customer's name and address are added only once. At that time discount percentage, credit limit, billing terms, and other information specific to that account are "keyboarded in." The customer is assigned a code name or number — "BD134" is the code we assigned to "B. Dalton

Bookseller Store #134," for example. (It's in the Puente Hills Mall, Pomona Freeway at Azusa, in beautiful City of Industry, California, for you bookstore trivia fans.)

For the purposes of this demonstration, however, let's create a mythical bookstore, The Mythical Bookstore. The customer code for The Mythical Bookstore is MYTH. Let's say The Mythical Bookstore sends in an order for five copies each of **The Personal Computer Book** and **The Word Processing Book**.

Standard accounting practices would require checking the credit rating of the store (do they have an outstanding balance due? Is it overdue? Does this order take them over their credit limit? What discount do they get?); filling out a shipping order; filling out a packing list; filling out a shipping label; figuring out the amount due; writing an invoice; recording the amount and date of invoice on the customer card; adding the amount of the sale to the daily order sheet (which will eventually be added to a periodic order sheet, which will eventually make its way to the general ledger); deducting the number of books ordered from the running inventory report (which eventually makes its way to the master inventory report); filing a copy of the invoice; and sending a copy of the invoice to The Mythical Bookstore.

With that amount of paperwork to ship ten (or two) books, it's little wonder that small publishers — like small businesses everywhere — find it, shall we say, a challenge, making ends meet.

With the PeachTree Invoice and Inventory programs, however, processing an order is quite a different matter.

To check the account's financial status, one types in "EC" for "Examine Credit." The program then asks for the customer code. We enter MYTH. In a moment, all the pertinent data concerning The Mythical Bookstore is displayed on the screen, including address, credit limit, date of last debit, amount of last debit, date of last credit, amount of last credit, year-to-date sales, year-to-date payments, and so on. (At this point, by the way, the human element comes irreplaceably into play: Should we send ten more books or should we not?)

One exits the Examine Credit mode by hitting the ESCAPE key (a key found on almost all personal computers that, as the name applies, will get you out of things). One then types "EN" for "ENter Invoices." (Yes, they do have an "ET." It's for "Enter Transactions.") Once again one is asked for the customer code. Again, we type in MYTH.

The date, which was keyboarded into the computer when it was first turned on earlier in the day, is automatically entered as the invoice date, although this date can be easily changed. (Whenever a program automatically selects something, it is known as the **default** setting. It saves adding frequently used parameters — such as dates in accounting or margins in word processing — over and over again. Defaults can generally be overridden by a simple command or two.)

The program remembers the last invoice number and assigns, as a default, the next available number. The shipping and billing address of the store are displayed, as are the discount, invoice date, terms, and so on. If all of this is acceptable, one moves to entering an invoice; if not, one can change anything on the screen.

Let's assume all the default settings and information from the customer file are accurate. To enter five copies of **The Word Processing Book**, one types the department code (which we have assigned as a dash, since we only have one department) and the product code ("WP" in the case of **The Word Processing Book**). One then enters the number of copies ordered (5) and moves onto the next title, **The Personal Computer Book**. The department is, again, " - " and the product code, in case you haven't guessed, is "PC." The number ordered, five, is entered, and the only remaining factor to add is the shipping charge. (The books are for resale, so they are not taxable.) The rest of the invoice — including all figuring — writes itself.

The entire invoice printed below was written using only the following commands: EN, MYTH, -WP, 5, -PC, 5, and 2.43.

```
Prelude Press
Box 69773
Los Angeles, California
90069
                                  INVOICE NO.: 575757

                                  INVOICE DATE: 11/26/82

                                       PAGE: 1


       The Mythical Bookstore              The Mythical Bookstore
SOLD 11011 Made Up Road             SHIP 11011 Made Up Road
 TO  Fabrication, Utah               TO  Fabrication, Utah
     12345                               12345


                                    CUSTOMER ID..: MYTH
                                    P.O. NUMBER..:
 SHIP VIA.:                         P.O. DATE....: 11/26/82
 SHIP DATE: 11/26/82                OUR ORDER NO.:
 DUE DATE.: 12/26/82                SALESMAN.....:
 TERMS....: 0-30-30


PRODUCT I.D.      DESCRIPTION     ORDERED   SHIPPED U/M UNIT PRICE   AMOUNT TX

 -  WP         Word Processing Book   5.00     5.00 EA     5.37       26.85
 -  PC         Pers. Computer Book    5.00     5.00 EA     5.37       26.85
FREIGHT        Shipping                                                2.43

                                            NET AMOUNT:              56.13
                                                   TAX:               0.00 *
                                            TOTAL DUE:               56.13
```

If that weren't enough, the program also removed five copies of each title from the inventory figures, posted the debit against the store, and recorded the entire trans-action in a temporary file that can later be added — auto-matically, of course — to the general ledger.

Similar descriptions of programs and the benefits they offer should be enough to coax all but the most critically cyberphobic into the computer age.

5. (Four was a long one, wasn't it?) Whenever possible, let the operators choose their own program. The choice of the computer itself is probably best left to The Boss for all those Boss-type reasons — cost, service, availability, do-I-

have-a-brother-in-law-in-the-computer-business — and it's a good idea to get the same make and model computer for everyone.

Fortunately, the more business-oriented personal computers do both accounting and word processing with equal ease. The peripherals for each machine might vary — accounting might require a hard disk while word processing might only need floppies, but word processing would require a letter-quality printer while accounting might only need a dot matrix — but the basic computer itself should be the same.

This allows for multiple-machine service contracts, second system discounts, employees feeling comfortable with each others's machines, the availability of at least one back-up computer during breakdowns, the ability of machines within an office to communicate more easily with each other, and so on.

The software, however, is another matter. Who knows better which accounting program will meet the company needs than The Bookkeeper? And who already knows more about the way words are processed in the office than The Secretary?

Personal computer programs that do the same things might do those things in very different ways. Personal computer programs have, yes, a personality, and that personality will have to interact with the personality of the person operating the program. It's best to let the person who will be interacting the most choose the program he or she will be interacting with.

Also, selecting an accounting or a word processing program is no easy matter, and being given the task will get a possibly reluctant employee more involved with the idea of personal computers long before the computer even arrives.

6. Give your employees time. Give them time to explore, compare, and select their programs. Give them time to read up on personal computers and their uses. Give them time to visit computer and software stores.

When I say give them time, I mean give them *paid* time. Give them one or two afternoons a week to do nothing but explore the land of computers. This might mean reading, this might mean visiting stores, this might mean lying down with a cold compress on the head. Let their readiness, their crystallization process, come in its own time — but let it come on company time.

When the computers and programs finally arrive, give them time to play with the computers, fiddle with them, learn the basics. Do not expect any output from the computer for a while. A program is a complicated — and often frustrating — thing to learn. If there is pressure from The Boss to turn out a trial balance or a mass mailing, well, you remember about the straws and the camels.

The best way to learn a program is by doing — trial and error — and in doing, some work might get accomplished, but don't rely on it. During training time, work will, in fact, be slower than usual. (Some recommend that a dual set of books — one on the computer and one on paper — be kept for at least six months *just in case*.)

7. Reward your workers for acquiring a new skill. This might mean a raise or an extended lunch hour or a bonus or however you wish to acknowledge that you have not only a Secretary and a Bookkeeper, but also two skilled Computer Operators as well.

Small computers are not just for small companies. More and more, personal computers are making their way into all levels of business, large and small.

In the executive suite, managers are finding that the financial services offered by The Dow Jones Service, Compu-Serve, and The Source to be invaluable. Like an answered prayer one never thought to pray, executives are peering into video screens from coast-to-coast and sighing, "How did I get along without it?"

The news, travel, stock quotations, research, shopping, and electronic mail features of the various data banks can be valuable and, every so often, a game or two might be in order.

The programs for the personal computers of

managers and executives is vast. After the success of VisiCalc, software vendors stumbled all over each other to offer not just electronic spreadsheets, but financial projection and business planning programs of all sorts and sizes.

These programs are designed to be run by the executive personally — not handed to an underling with the instructions, "Run these figures through the computer." The difference between direct contact with the program, and being one or more levels removed is remarkable. Direct contact encourages fiddling, nudging, experimenting, trial runs, and the sort of creative fooling around that sometimes results in a work of genius.

"Hands on" computer operation in the executive suite also removes the time lag between the idea and the "numbers." Figures can be figured on the spot — no two hour or two day wait while someone visits the mainframe.

Once executives become comfortable with their personal computer, they might even try a little (shhh) word processing. Few will admit to it, of course. Typing is for typists, not for bosses. However, a great many people find that their thoughts are not as clearly communicated through dictation as through the more traditional method of pen-to-paper. Most of these executives will find that writing on a personal computer is even more productive than writing by hand.

Someone once said that if correspondence is a part of your job, you are a professional writer. There are few professional writers I know who can successfully dictate. Most try it out, but return to the pen or the keyboard. It seems to work better that way. Many executives who try word processing find that they prefer it to dictation for important letters, proposals, and reports.

Most people tend to overwrite, and the speed with which one can remove the excess on a personal computer is remarkable. More about this in the chapter on word processing.

Outside the executive suite, personal computers are finding a home on other levels of big business as well. Various departments in charge of this or that find a personal computer programmed to do this or that as useful as the adding machine is to the accountant or the typewriter is to the secretary.

Cost projections, amortizations, research, airline reservations — the list is endless. Chances are, whatever a department does, there's a computer program — on disks or in a data bank — that will help do it better, faster, and easier.

Word processing is one of the things personal computers do best. Every expensive electric typewriter you see is a perfect place for a personal computer running a word processing program. The reasons for this are detailed in the next chapter on word processing, but let's consider for a moment word processing specifically in the large corporation.

Here, reprinted from **The Word Processing Book**, are six reasons why twenty personal computers with word processing programs *might* be a better buy for a large corporation than one large computer with twenty terminals.

1. It takes a long time, a lot of money, and an unbearable amount of expert consultation to decide which large computer to buy. Further, it is often difficult to justify the expense of buying a large computer for word processing alone. Higher-ups will say "Well, we already have a computer. Let's use that one." The computer in the data processing department may be ill suited for word processing, or may be too small to add a dozen extra terminals. And how do you prove it will do any good once you got the big computer? This takes yet another study, and another study takes more time and more money. And on and on and on.

Buying a personal computer or two, and having them replace a Selectric or two, is not difficult. Within six months you'll have information, from within your own company, on how they are doing. If the results are positive, then several more machines can be added. If the results are favorable six months later, you can get a word processing computer for everyone. It'll take a year, but that will be less time than most corporations spend researching and buying a large computer.

"And then we're going to put the printer over there in that building.
Would you like to see?"

2. There is a fear of computers among some office workers. In starting slow, you can give word processors to those who are anxious to have them. They will use them well, the fearful will learn that there is nothing to fear, and within a brief period of time, the formerly frightened will be demanding a computer of their own.

3. How often have you heard the phrase "Our computer is down?" Like most of us, computers do "get down" from time to time. If twenty people are dependent upon one computer for all their word processing needs, you can imagine what happens when the one computer stops working. If, however, you have twenty separate computers, and one breaks, it's hardly noticed. In larger corporations, having an extra word processing computer "in reserve" would be a justifiable — if not intelligent — expense.

Why couldn't they offer the choice, "experienced and clean?"

4. Since a word processing computer is nothing more than a personal computer programmed for word processing, it is very easy to run other programs and have the computer do almost anything else. One executive, for example, might need to have accurate stock market quotations. Another executive might find financial projections using one of the many electronic spreadsheet programs invaluable. A third might need ongoing airline information, a fourth might use electronic mail, and so on.

Rather than a terminal attached to an inflexible large computer, you have the advantage of many small computers and the flexibility they offer.

5. If it happens all at once, the transition from individual typewriters to one large computer can be a nightmare. The addition of individual word processors can take place gradually, over a period of time, and the overall workflow of the office need not be disturbed.

6. Twenty personal computers, complete with printers and word processing software would, at $7,000 per computer, cost $140,000. You can *easily* spend that much money researching, purchasing, and programming a large 20 terminal computer.

There are situations in which it is far more economical to buy one large computer. I mention the advantages of individual word processing computers because, if you call in a word processing expert who has spent the last ten years installing nothing but large-scale word processing operations, it is doubtful that he or she will mention any of the above. It is, in fact, possible that he or she might not even *know* any of the above. Personal computers have been around for very few years. Many of the Big Computer experts continue to look upon them as toys.

But toys they are not. Personal computers are tools, and it's been a long time since a tool as varied, versatile, and infinitely useful to the business community has come along.

The Wonders of
Word Processing

The Basics of Word Processing

Discussing word processing is like discussing Beethoven's Fifth Symphony. There are a great many recordings of this symphony, all different. Some are less different than others. The several versions done by the New York Philharmonic are going to be more similar to each other than the one done by the Omaha All Kazoo Band.

And so it is with word processing programs. There are about as many word processing programs as there are recordings of Beethoven's Fifth — maybe more. They're all different, but some are less different than others. The ones costing $500 are likely to be more similar to each other than are the ones costing $19.95.

All recordings of Beethoven's Fifth, from the Berliner Philharmonic to the Tijuana Symphony will begin with (we hope) "DA DA DA DUM." So, too, (we hope) do all word processing programs have some things in common. Let's look at those similarities, the basic features you can expect from any word processing program. Then we'll discuss the many variations, additions, and refinements that ingenious programmers have added in the past few years.

In explaining a basic word processing program, I'll use the typewriter for comparison. When you type on a typewriter, the words are transferred directly to the paper. When you type on a computer, the words appear on the video screen. Rather than ink on paper, you have written with electrons on phosphor. Ink on paper is hard to change; electrons on phosphor, easy.

If you make a mistake on a typewriter and catch it before putting too many characters between you and the mistake, you have several correcting options. The first is an eraser. Not recommended. The next is paint; little jars of white paint with brushes in them. You paint over the mistake, let it dry, and type over the paint. Similarly, there are little sheets of white carbon paper that will hide mistakes, in a fashion.

The ultimate solution to typing errors was the Wonder of the Age back in 1974: The IBM Correcting Selectric. On this machine you push a button, backspace to the mistake, retype the mistake, and a ribbon of flypaper comes out of the typewriter and magically lifts the offending characters right off the page! Why, this so thrilled typists throughout the country that there was a movement to give IBM Thursday of National Secretary's Week.

To make a correction on a word processor you press the "delete" button and watch it erase all that went before it, letter by letter until you release the button. You then type in, or "keyboard in" as they say in Computerese, whatever you would prefer to have in that space.

Let's say you've finished typing a page, and it comes fresh and neat from the typewriter. You notice a sentence in the middle of the page that should not be there. Another sentence, that happens to be quite a bit longer than the sentence that should not be there, should be there. What do you have? A Moral Dilemma. A question worthy of Aristotle arises: "Is making this change that should be made worth retyping the whole page?" And if it's a long document, several pages long, and the pages have already been typed, the change would mean going onto another page, so the question becomes, "Is making this change that should be made worth retyping the whole document?"

If you own a word processor, you need never face that dilemma again. You will have to face other dilemmas, like how to pay for the word processor perhaps, but you will never face the to-retype-or-not-to-retype dilemma again. Whatever you're working on in word processing, from a wedding invitation to the great American novel, is known as a document. When you want to make a change in a document, you move the cursor to the point in the document where the change is to be made, and make it. A cursor is a little, blinking square that is the length and height of one letter —it tells you where you are in the document.

Taking words out, putting words in, correcting spelling, removing or adding literally pages of information can take place at any point in the document. The rest of the document adjusts accordingly, automatically, electronically. Change is easy because it's all done with electrons and electrons *love* to change. You could say it is one of their primary characteristics.

This ability to change what you want to change whenever you want to change it is the key to the value and growing popularity of word processing computers. With this feature, even the most basic word processing program can do more than the most expensive and sophisticated type-directly-onto-a-piece-of-paper typewriter.

After everything looks all right on the video screen, it comes time to print. Even the slowest printer types faster than all but the fastest typists, and printers can do it hour after hour after hour, 24 hours a day if necessary. The slower computer printers (converted IBM Selectrics, ironically enough) print at 15 characters per second (CPS).

Figuring an average word to be seven letters long (that's just my figuring; heaven knows the length of an average word), that comes to 128.57 words per minute (WPM). The slower printers designed especially for computers print at 25 CPS or about 215 WPM; and the faster letter-perfect printers for computers travel at the remarkable rate of 55 CPS, which clocks in at around 470 words per minute. They print in both directions, from left to right and then, not to waste a return trip, from right to left. Many dot matrix printers go faster than that.

As you might gather, even if changes are desired after the document has been printed, making changes on the video screen and then printing a new document requires minimal time and effort. In fact, while doing word processing, working copies are printed all the time. The onus on retyping and re-retyping, and even re-re-retyping is gone. Push a few buttons and the printer clicks out a new copy in a matter of minutes.

The implication this has on personalized form letters is obvious. You can send out hundreds of letters, all saying the same thing, each looking hand typed, and the only thing you need to change each time is the name. And, fellow writers: Freshly typed manuscripts are far more impressive than Xerox copies.

Those are the basics you can expect from any system that dares call itself a word processor. Although formidable, it's just the beginning.

Some people require or desire a feature or two or twelve more than a basic word processing program provides. Who can blame them? After spending several thousand dollars on hardware, spending a few hundred more on better quality software that will turn their Volkswagen into a Mercedes is certainly understandable.

What follows is a guide to some of the features designers of word processing software have created. Each description will begin with the Computerese name for the feature.

File Length. File length determines how long a document can be. This is usually designated by the number of **K** or **Kilobytes**, each kilobyte being equal to 1024 **bytes**. A letter, number, character, or space is a **byte**. "20K" would be around 20,000 bytes, "240K" would be about 240,000 bytes, etc. If you're wondering what the relationship between a kilobyte and the written word is, a double-spaced, type-written, 8½ x 11 sheet of paper with generous margins contains about 2,000 bytes, or 2K. Some less expensive word processing programs can handle only one or two pages of text at a time. (Of course, longer documents can be done one page at a time, just like on a typewriter.) The finest word processing software limits the size of the document to "disk capacity," meaning that, however many K the disk is capable of holding, that is the maximum length of the document.

Word Wrap. This means that when you reach the end of the line (meaning right-hand margin, not major life crisis), the next word will begin the next line automatically.

This may take some getting used to. If you're accustomed to a manual typewriter, you may find your left hand moving suddenly upwards and slapping the side of the video screen at the end of each line. Once you've become adjusted to word wrap, however, it's delightful. No more listening for the little bell. No more looking up to see how much room is left on a line. No more wondering if the next word will fit before the carriage stops dead. No more margin releases. Just type, type, type. The only time you'd use the carriage return is to begin a new paragraph or when you want the line to end before the right margin, such as in list making or poetry writing.

File Insertion. Each disk has many files. A file can be anywhere from one letter in length to the maximum length permitted by the word processing program. If you were typing along on file A, and you wanted to add the contents of files B, C, and D to file A, with the push of a few buttons it would be done.

Using file insertion you could create files of frequently used paragraphs or phrases and have them added to the text in a matter of seconds. This is great for correspondence or contracts. I have my name and address in a file marked AD and my name, address and phone number in a file marked ADP. When I come to the end of a letter and want to add my name and address I type two letters — a code to let the computer know that I want to "read" a file into my text — and then type AD. If I wanted to include my phone number I would type ADP. Zip. There it is.

Block Move. A block is a group of words that are all together in a bunch. I guess if you drew straight lines around a chosen bit of text on a printed page it would look like a block. I don't know. The logic of those three people who sat up until four in the morning making up these terms escapes me. At any rate, if you've ever written a paragraph and then wished it were in another part of the document, you will appreciate block moves.

All you'd need do is mark the beginning of the block, the end of the block, move the cursor to where you'd like that block to go, and within seconds the block has moved into its new neighborhood feeling very much at home. There are other good things you can do with blocks:

Copy Blocks, which lets you make a copy of the block, so that the original block stays where it is, but an identical copy can be written into another part of the document.

You can also copy a block onto another file. Let's say you're typing along and discover you have written a paragraph that you will want to use again in other documents. You can copy it onto a new file, naming it whatever you like, and move on. The next time you need that paragraph, you can use file insertion and read it into the text. All this moving around of blocks, by the way, is known as "text manipulation."

Global Search. Although this sounds like something James Bond might request ("We'll find him, sir. I'll have a global search run on him right away"), global search in word processing is far less dramatic, although equally exciting. Global search will find anything, at any point in your document, in a matter of seconds.

Let's say you have a very long document, and you want to return to the section in which you were rhapsodizing about clouds. You would simply type the word "cloud" into global search, and the computer would find and display the first time you used that word. If that wasn't quite the section you wanted, with the push of a button the computer would move to the point in your document where "cloud" was used for the second time, and so on.

Search and Replace. This not only finds any word or character in the document, it will change that word or character to any other word or character. If you've written a letter to Michael, using his name throughout the letter, and now you want to send the same letter to Mary, all you do is have the computer find each occurrence of "Michael" and change it to "Mary." In a few seconds the letter will be personalized to Mary.

Another use for search and replace is to save typing. Let's suppose you're doing a very long report on the heterobasidiomycetes (a subclass of fungi, for the two or three out there who didn't know. You know who you are). Now, writing as you would be on heterobasidiomycetes, you would no doubt have to mention the word heterobasidiomycetes quite often. You might not want to type out heterobasidiomycetes as many times as you'd be using heterobasidiomycetes, and you may, in fact, after awhile, find yourself avoiding the word heterobasidiomycetes altogether. Now, rather than type out the word heterobasidiomycetes each time, with search and replace all you would have to do is use an abbreviation, say "H" each time you wanted to use heterobasidiomycetes. When finished you would simply have search and replace find all occurrences of "H" and replace them with "heterobasidiomycetes." In this way your report, your fingers, and your sanity are saved by search and replace.

Dictionary. (Also known as Proofreader or Spell Check or something along those lines.) This checks every word in your document against a list of correctly spelled words. These lists of correctly spelled words range from 10,000 to 45,000 words. If a word in your document does not match a word in the word list, it means that either the word is misspelled or the word is correctly spelled but not located in the program's list of words.

The dictionary feature will make a list of the unmatched words for you to examine. If they are correctly spelled, they can be added to the dictionary. All future checks will include those words. If they are incorrectly spelled, they are automatically marked in the text and found using global search. (A "*" for example, is placed by the program before each misspelled word. You have global search find all incidences of the symbol "*" and, one by one, the misspelled words will present themselves for correction.) Incorrect spellings, by the way, include most typographical errors. This feature is great for ferreting out typing mistakes, the ones usually discovered *after* the letter is sent.

Most often this feature will not be found as part of a word processing program, but can be purchased as a separate program and used with whatever word processing software you own. The best dictionary programs will look up the correct spelling for a word, even if you don't know how it's spelled. You type in how you think it's spelled and, nine times out of ten, it will come up with the correct spelling. (The next chapter, **The Curse of Noah Webster** looks at one of these dictionary programs in greater detail.)

Centering. The computer will automatically center any word or group of words between the left and right margins. Great for headings, titles, addresses, invitations, poetry, and the like.

Page Display. This will display on the video screen where the page breaks will be when the document is printed. It helps avoid the last three words of a paragraph beginning a new page.

Automatic Pagination. The page numbers will automatically be printed at the bottom, top, left, or right side of every page. Like most features, this one can be "switched off" so that no page numbers print.

Screen Oriented. Programs that are screen oriented mean that what you see on the video screen is what you'll get on the printed page. If you want justified right margins, they will be displayed that way on the screen. If you make a change, that change is reflected instantly on the screen in both the content of the words and the format the words are in.

Word processing programs that are not screen oriented are known as **character oriented**. This means you see all the words displayed in the order, but not necessarily in the format, that they will be printed. Some people don't mind this. As long as one word follows another as written and the new paragraphs begin when requested, that's all that matters. Others will want to see what they're working on, in the form it will be printed, as they go.

Justification. No, this is not a list of good excuses for why you spent so much money on a fancy typewriter. This means the right margin is straight and even, just like the left. Most books, newspapers and magazines use justified right and left margins, also known as "flush right" and "flush left."

Studies have shown, however, that while perfectly justified right and left margins look more impressive on a printed page, unjustified ("ragged") right margins are easier to read. Moral: If you want to impress, turn the justification on. If you want to communicate, turn it off. (And you can see where *this* book stands!)

Justification is done by expanding shorter lines. This expansion is done by adding spaces. If little itsy-bitsy-teeny-tiny spaces are added between letters, this is known as **microspacing.**

Proportional Spacing. A typewriter allots the same amount of space for each letter, so that a capital "W" is the same width as a small "i." Proportional spacing prints the "W" wider than an "a" and an "a" wider than an "i." Most books and magazines print with proportional spacing. Proportional spacing produces printed copy that is as close as you can get to professional typesetting. This requires, of course, not only the appropriate software but also one of the better letter quality printers.

While we're on the subject of printers, why don't we wind up this review of word processing capabilities with some of the many printing enhancements that are available when a first-rate printer and top-quality word processing program combine. In fact, let's switch from professional phototypesetting to a letter quality word processing printer.

Underlining. We all know what underlining is. At least I hope we all know what underlining is. Underlining is when you draw a line under something. The words "hope" and "under" were underlined, as was the word "underlined." (Do you see how boring this book must be to anyone who knows a lot about word processing?)

Double Strike. This means that every character is typed twice. It gives a darker, more solid impression and would stand out on a page, but not quite as blatantly as boldface. It is very useful for preparing copy that is later to be printed.

Boldface. Here, too, each character is typed twice, but the second impression is slightly to one side of the first. The "slightly" is very slight, so that the two impressions overlap and form one dark, solid character.

Pitch Changes. This refers to how many characters there are per inch. The pitches we're most accustomed to are pica, which is ten characters per inch, and elite, twelve characters per inch. The better programs and printers allow you to change from one to another, at any point, without interrupting the printing. At least one system can print as few as four characters per inch, and as many as thirty. Thirty characters per inch. As my father would say, "Can you feature that?" Well, all right, I will feature that. Here is what "Come live with me and be my love and we will all the pleasures prove" looks like at thirty characters per inch:

Cce lievitne acbery be acvevill all tepleausproe.

Subscript and **Superscript.** These functions put the words, characters or numbers slightly below or slightly above the line they are printed on. It's useful when writing H_2O

(the "2" is in subscript) or $E=MC^2$ (the "2" is in superscript.)

Kerning. Kerning is a term from printing that refers to the spacing between letters. Some word processing software allows the movement of a single letter to the right or to the left in infinitesimal increments.

Overprinting. This allows you to print one character over another. It's useful in foreign languages, when you want to put the "'" over the "e" in "olé" or if you want to create your own characters, as someone did when he combined the "?" with the "!" and came up with "‽". It's called an interrobang and it's used to punctuate sentences such as "You're what‽" or "You're going where‽" or "You just bought a word processing what‽"

Strikeout. For the life of me I cannot see the point of strikeout. All it does is put little dashes (-----) over whatever you've written and prints it that way. You pay all this money for a word processing machine so that there will never have to be any more strikeouts or erasures or white carbon paper or white paint all over your documents and then they include a special way of making them look bad. I don't know. The only possible use I can come up with is to make typewriter-like mistakes so that no one will know you have a word processing machine and nobody will want to come over and use it. That's all I can figure. (I am told this has some value in a law office. A great many unusual things do.)

The text above is an example of proportionally spaced printing on a word processor. The text you are reading now is an example of nonproportional (regular) spacing. With regular spacing, each letter is allowed the same amount of room, no matter how wide or narrow it might be. This is standard for typewriters. The type faces are designed, in fact, so that an "i" is wider than it might normally be and an "M" is narrower.

This paragraph and the one just above are also set with right-and-left justified margins (obviously) using microspacing. The spaces necessary to extend shorter lines to the right margin are added in between each letter rather than in between each word.

The look of a printed document is also affected by the choice of type styles and how those type styles are manipulated. This is the same typeface as the previous two paragraphs, but the pitch was changed from 10 to 12 pitch. In this way the same print wheel gives different results.

Print wheels can be changed, of course, and a wide variety of type styles is available. We just switched from Courier to Times Roman. The proportional spacing above was printed in Emperor. Some word processing programs allow for print wheel changes *within* sentences. This allows one to *italicize* words by changing type wheels. **Boldface** does not require changing type wheels since it is done **automatically** by the printer and the word processing program.

For most correspondence you'll want people to think it was typed on a regular (albeit expensive electric) typewriter. You'll probably want to turn the right justification off. If you send out left-and-right justified letters people will know you have a word processor and suspect form paragraphs ---or worse---form letters. To maintain the illusion, you can print correspondence ragged right.

This chapter has exhausted only you and me. It has far from exhausted all the features currently available on word processing programs, and more are coming every day. Whatever your personal needs involving the processing of words, the chances are good that the program exists that will make your task a whole lot easier. If they can help me spell, they can do anything.

The Curse of Noah Webster

I have always had a fondness for Thomas Jefferson. Anyone who wrote the Declaration of Independence and said, "I have nothing but contempt for anyone who can spell a word only one way," can't be all bad. I will not be spending much time on the Declaration of Independence in this chapter, but I have a feeling that I will be discussing the subject of spelling a great deal.

I am an awful speller. I am so bad that I don't even know when a word is spelled correctly. Ninety percent of the words I take the time to look up (and I do mean time: I'm lousy at alphabetical order, too) are right in the first place. It's discouraging. Hence, one of the deciding factors in my purchase of a computer with word processing capabilities was the flurry of programs promising to forever end the Curse of Noah Webster. (He's the one who started it all, you know. He's the one who came along 198 years ago and gave Americans only one way to spell a word. The right way. His way.)

In my research I came across a bit of dictionary software that not only does more than any of the others I've used or read about, but costs less. Far less.

The WORD retails for $75. (Spellguard, the trade name for another popular spelling-correction program, costs $295. Others run in the $200-250 range.) "The first question people ask me," says the creator of The WORD, Wayne Holder, "is 'What's wrong with it? Why is it so cheap?'" Thus far I've found nothing "wrong," and a good deal right, with it.

I will use a description of The WORD's several programs as the basis for this chapter. Not only will it tell you what is available in dictionary software today, but it will show you how special features can be added to whatever word processing program you decide upon.

The dictionary in The WORD is massive, more than 45,000 words. The dictionary is compressed, allowing that many words, plus all other programs and commands, to fit into less than 154K of disk space. (The dictionary uses 136K of that.)

The WORD will do what all the other "dictionary" programs will do, namely check each word in the text against the correctly spelled words in the dictionary; list words that do not match (indicating misspellings, typos, uncommon proper names, jargon or technical terms); and then, after the option to edit the list, mark the mismatched words in the text for correction.

The latest edition of The WORD (version 2.0) uses a feature called REVIEW. Each of the mismatched words appears, one by one, and with a single keystroke you can either mark the misspelled word in the text for later correction; add the word, if correctly spelled, to the dictionary so the word will never appear on a mismatched word list again; add the correctly spelled word to a special dictionary that will only be checked upon request; or delete the word from the mismatch list altogether.

What if you accidentally delete a word that should have been added to the dictionary, or add a word to the dictionary that should have been marked as a misspelling? Review is very forgiving. You simply back up and reroute the word to its desired location. (If you have a version of The WORD prior to 2.0, OASIS will update it for only $10.)

To find the correct spelling for the misspelled words, The WORD uses a program descriptively entitled LOOKUP. LOOKUP is a tool that, from my point of view, is worth far more than $75 all by itself. One simply types "LOOKUP" and the way one *thinks* the word should be spelled, and LOOKUP will, nine times out of ten, find the correct spelling. I misspelled twelve words in the writing of this chapter, and LOOKUP found the acceptable-to-Mr.-Webster spelling for eleven of them.

It does this, I am told, by "correcting" the word in a great many ways, using the four most common mistakes in spelling, checking these "corrections" against the main dictionary, and listing the words that match. All this takes about ten seconds.

If I were to ask it to LOOKUP THIER, for example, The WORD would list THEIR, THIEF and TIER. I may be bad at spelling, but of the three, I known the word I'm looking for is THEIR.

A problem in any spell-check program is homophones. Homophones are words that are pronounced the same but spelled differently, depending on their use: words like "stationary" and "stationery"; "their," "they're," and "there"; "to," "too," and "two." Take the sentence: "Their going two the stationary store, to." Although this sentence would sound all right if it were spoken, and although individual words are correctly spelled, because of each word's usage there are four misspellings in that sentence. "They're going to the stationery store, too." would be correct. Since dictionary programs can only check the spelling of words, and not their context in a sentence, homophones are a problem.

The WORD offers a partial solution to this problem. The program has a file of 860 homophones. You go through and remove the homophones you know how to use correctly. The ones that remain are potential troublemakers for you, and The WORD will, upon request, mark these words in the text for closer review.

Another fascinating feature of The WORD, indispensable to crossword puzzle fanatics (who don't mind a little help) and writers who need to rhyme (who welcome all the help they can get), is FIND. Based upon the number of letters known, with "?" or "*" representing the letters unknown, FIND will find all the words that might fit the format you request. If, for example, you were doing a crossword puzzle and you needed a four-letter word that ended in "Q," all you'd need do is type "FIND ???Q" (each "?" represents one letter), and in less than a minute FIND would tell you that the word you're most likely looking for is "IRAQ."

If you were writing an "Ode To My Computer" and were seeking a melodic match for "terminal," all you'd do to find more than enough rhymes is enter "FIND *AL" ("*" represents any number of letters) and all words, of any length, ending in "AL" would come flooding forth (as a poet might say). This would give a nearly endless list of words. To tighten the rhyme you might want to remove just the first letter and enter "FIND *ERMINAL." This yields only one possibility, GERMINAL. So you might want to loosen the rhyme a bit and leave off the first syllable, entering "FIND *MINAL." This brings forth from the depths of iron oxide such gems as CRIMINAL, NOMINAL and SEMINAL.

Two more great tools for the writer included in The

WORD are Wordcount (WC) and Word Frequency (WORD-FREQ). There are 2,099 words in this chapter. It took Wordcount about three seconds to give me that information. (Can you imagine how long it would have taken me to give me that information?) However, there are only 611 unique words. That is, I used 611 words, and by repeating some, came up with a 2,099-word chapter. Which words were repeated, and how many times each? That's where Word Frequency comes in.

Word Frequency tells how many times each word in the document was used, and will list them either in descending order of usage or alphabetically. The Top Ten words in this chapter are: **THE** (with a whopping 165 occurrences), **WORD** (with 76), **AND** edged out **A** (with 55 and 54 respectively), **IN** (53), **OF** (51), **TO** (47), **FOR** (35), **IS** (30) and, egomaniac that I am, I used **I** 29 times. Of the 611 unique words, 349 of them were used only once.

So, I used 611 words, 349 only once, repeated 262 of them as many as 165 times each to form a 2,099-word chapter. Now where else in the world could I come up with that information?

DICTSORT (Dictionary Sorter) is a program that will put any group of words in alphabetical order within seconds. If it puts one index of one book in order, it's paid for itself. Also great for mailing lists, record collections (mine is: Popular, alphabetical by artist; Classical, alphabetical by composer), or, if you're more like Daniel Webster than Noah Webster, it will put your book of "Alternative Spellings for Free Americans" in perfect order faster than you can say, "Life, liberty and the pursuit of happiness."

Each 5¼-inch disk on my word processing computer will hold about 340K of information. I've combined The WORD with WordStar (a word processing program described in Chapter Thirteen), along with a few of my own boilerplate paragraphs, on one disk and I still have 80K to spare. I use this disk for correspondence, articles, or short chapters. I enter text, edit, correct spelling, and print, all without changing drives. I then copy the file onto an appropriate storage disk, erase the original, and have 80K again for my next project.

The WORD is fast. With my system, spelling is checked on shorter documents in under a minute. I clocked an 8,382 word document at one minute and nineteen seconds, a 10,535 word document in one minute and forty-nine seconds. It would take me an hour to read, much less proofread, a 10,535 word document!

The 42-page manual is clear, friendly, and to the point. It includes all you'll need to know to be working The WORD within an hour. (Maybe less for you: I'm as bad at reading as I am at spelling.)

I can heartily recommend any of the several programs contained in The WORD for the $75 price; and when they're all together, in one package, at that same price, well, it's one of the great software bargains around.

Some people can't leave well enough alone. Wayne Holder seems to be one of these people. Not content with a perfectly good spell-check program, he had to go and improve it. The result is The WORD Plus. If you were happy with The WORD, you'll be ecstatic with The WORD Plus.

The WORD Plus is **menu driven**. A menu in personal computing is the same as a menu in a restaurant: It lists all that's available. Menu driven also means the programs, or portions of the programs, will be presented in a logical order for selection. In a restaurant this logical order might be appetizer, soup, salad, main course, dessert.

In a spell-check program, the first logical question would be, "Which file would you like checked?" This is The WORD Plus's first question. One types in the name of the file and hits the return key. The WORD Plus checks the file for misspellings, tells you how many there are, and then automatically goes into the REVIEW program.

As described earlier in this chapter, the REVIEW program presents words not found in the 45,000-word dictionary one at a time for, well, review.

One can delete the word from the misspelled list, add the word to the dictionary, or mark the word in the text. With The WORD Plus, one has several other choices. One can, for example, ask for the context in which the word appeared. If the misspelled word is "ands," should it have been "and," "ends," "sands," or one of several other possible words? Looking at the misspelled word alone, it's hard to tell. With the press of one button (the V key for "View"), The WORD Plus displays the line from the original text in which the word appears.

After discovering that the word should be "and," one pushes the C key (for "correct") and types "AND." The WORD Plus will, wonder of wonders, change "ands" to "and" in the text. No need to mark the word with an asterisk and return to the text and change it; the correction takes place automatically.

The WORD Plus incorporates the LOOKUP feature in REVIEW. Simply push L and within a few seconds (less than five on my computer), several possible correct spellings for the misspelled word are listed. With two keystrokes the correct word is noted and the acceptable-to-Mr.-Webster spelling automatically replaces the misspelled word in the text.

Two features, not directly connected to spelling correction, but helpful in the processing of words, are a part of The WORD Plus. The first is HYPHEN. As the names implies, this program will either suggest possible hyphenations for individual words, or place "soft hyphens" in all the words in a given text. Soft hyphens are hyphens that print as hyphens only when they fall at the end of a line, otherwise the words print whole without hyphenation. This is invaluable in documents with narrow margins, long words, or both.

The second, almost for fun, is called ANAGRAM. This will find anagrams for any word or collection of letters — provided, of course, that the anagrams to be found are listed in the 45,000-word dictionary. (An anagram of ANIMAL is MANILA, for example. Anagrams for SAINT include STAIN and SATIN.)

Beyond solving word-scramble puzzles and finding character names that subconsciously hint at personality traits, ANAGRAM will find words based upon *sounds*.

Let's say you were writing a story and wanted to set the mood with ooo sounds, like soothing or smooth. One would simply type in "ANAGRAM OO???" and all five-letter words with two Os would appear — a long list with BLOOM,

MOONS and ROMEO among them. How about all six letter words with three Os? Type "ANAGRAM OOO???" and one discovers such beautiful words as COCOON, ROCOCO and COMORO (a group of Islands in the Mozambique Channel).

If you wanted to find some buzz words, I mean real buzz words, words with some zip and pizzazz to them, you could type in "ANAGRAM ZZ???" and be pelted with DIZZY, FRIZZ and JAZZY. Harder sounding words? Let's try "ANAGRAM KK???." We're assaulted with KHAKI, KINKY and our old friend KODAK.

The WORD Plus sells for $150, half as much as the best-selling spell-check program, although The WORD Plus does much, much more. Those who own The WORD can upgrade to The WORD Plus for $75.

The WORD Plus approaches perfection in spell-check programs; it certainly is the state of the art. But some people can leave neither perfection nor the state of the art alone....

(to be continued.)

This early word processor required two adults and a small child to operate. The keyboard is left, video screen in the center, printer on the right.

"FINE LARGE CUCUMBERS!"

Word Processing
and the Single Bookseller

In the small town of Prospect, Ohio, Mrs. Wicks owns and operates Wicks Book Store. Although her inventory is one-fourth that of the Big City bookstore just down the street, Mrs. Wicks sells more books than they do. This is because Mrs. Wicks cares about every book and every person that goes through her store.

Mrs. Wicks, a retired school teacher, loves books. She loves people, too, especially people who love books. Her gift is remembering what subjects her customers like and notifying them of new titles as they become available.

As more and more people let Mrs. Wicks know their areas of interest, she began cross-referencing these in a card file. Eventually she got a computer. "It was either hire someone or buy a computer." Mrs. Wicks explains. "I decided I'd get on better with a computer."

Mrs. Wicks carefully reads all publishers' catalogs and book announcements in *Publisher's Weekly* and the *Ingram Trade Advance*. Popular books she orders, and when they arrive she sends out personalized letters announcing their arrival to interested readers:

> Borta O'Hara's latest novel, "Love's Mad, Tender, Passionate Embrace of Torrid Desire" is now in stock. This is Ms. O'Hara's first book since "Passion's Potent Potion," which came out last week, and is said to be her best novel since last month's "Rapture Erupts." Due in next Friday: "Uncle Tom's Passion."

For books with limited appeal, Mrs. Wicks sends a letter informing the customers that the book is in print and can be special ordered:

> The latest book on health food, "Don't Eat Yogurt---They Put Bacteria in It!" is now in print and I can order it for you. Chapters include "MSG and the CIA," "Go Yeast Young Man" and "How to Make Solar Granola."

Mrs. Wicks has her word processor print out reply cards, which are included with each letter. These have the titles of the books suggested, the customer's name and address, and possible methods of payment.

The customer, after reading the letter, need only check the appropriate boxes and place the return reply card in the return reply envelope, thoughtfully — and cleverly — enclosed by Mrs. Wicks.

This is the return mail card of Mr. John Doe, a man who, according to Mrs. Wicks's computer, likes books on cooking, Watergate, sex education, and making money:

Dear Mrs. Wicks, Please send me:

_____ copies "Joy of Cooking Sex" ($9.95)

_____ copies "I Know How to Be Really Rich and You Don't" ($25.00)

_____ copies "The Last Whole Nixon Catalog" ($1.75)

_____ Please bill to my account.

_____ Check enclosed

Charge to my

_____ Visa _____ MasterCard

Number: _____

Expiration Date: _____

_____ Mail books to me.

_____ Hold books at the store.

_____ Call me when they arrive.

Thank you very much.

John Doe

123 Main Street

Anytown, Ohio

12345

Although her inventory is several hundred thousand dollars less than the Big City bookstore down the street, is it any wonder that Mrs. Wicks and her $6,000 word processing computer sometimes get the feeling that they are the only bookstore in town?

" FRESH OYSTERS ! PENNY A LOT ! "

I could sit here imagining word processing applications for imaginary businesses all night — come to think of it, I already have. If you are self-employed, I invite you to join in this brainstorming with me: If you had a machine that did all the things described in this book sitting in front of you right now, how might it benefit your business? How might it help you serve those for whom you do your work? How might it make you, or someone who works for you, more productive? How might it help you generate more business? How might it help you organize the business you already have?

Word processing computers are not magic wands. They will not, in and of themselves, save a dying company. They will not turn a poor business person into an entrepreneur.

A word processor is a powerful tool that, when used with intelligence and creativity, will lead the self-employed individual several steps closer to the goals of success, abundance, and personal freedom.

"PINS, NEW PINS!"

The Drawbacks of Personal Computers

Yes, there are drawbacks to personal computers, and I'll tell you what they are. You won't have to hear it first from Geraldo Rivera on a *20/20* expose.

There are drawbacks to everything, of course, and drawbacks must be weighed in proportion to benefits. Further, most drawbacks can be reduced or eliminated if approached creatively. So, in this chapter, we will be looking not only at problems, but also at solutions.

Here they are then, the several drawbacks (and suggested remedies) to personal computers I have encountered.

1. Computers are expensive. Personal computers cost a lot in terms of both time and money. Some people I know have enough money, but they don't have much time. Some people I know have enough time, but don't have much money. Most people I know have neither enough time nor enough money. Personal computers require a sizeable investment of both.

Will this investment pay off? Will it be worth it? Like installing a swimming pool, it's hard to know until you take the plunge. Health clubs could not exist without the remarkably high drop-out rate of their members. Fully 80% of the people who join, signing up for several years at several hundred dollars, never go near the place after the first month. If everyone who joined made use of the facilities, health clubs would be five times more crowded than they are now, a burden they would be unable to bear.

A personal computer is something that you will buy, use a few times, and then abandon, a monument to your impulsiveness and lack of determination — like a Cuisinart. Or, you will buy a personal computer, wonder how you ever got along without it, and use it daily for a variety of tasks you would never dream of doing again by hand, a living example of your good taste and practical nature — like a Cuisinart.

Recommending that you "start small" doesn't help

much. As those who bought a discounted version of a Cuisinart will tell you, most of the knock-offs were no bargain — they butchered meat rather than sliced it, and mangled vegetables rather than chopped them. The very people who might have been happy with a *genuine* Cuisinart, found the imitator unacceptable, assumed the praise heaped upon food processors was grossly overstated, and returned to the processing of food by more traditional methods.

If you want, for example, to do word processing, and attempt it on a $300 machine, you might find it unsatisfactory; whereas, if you were to attempt it on an $1,800 machine, you might be thrilled; and if you were to try word processing on a $5,000 machine, you might find yourself unable to write even a shopping list without it.

If you don't process words (or do bookkeeping, or have a passion for electronic games, or one of the other things that personal computers do remarkably well), it's hard to know if the many things that personal computers do marginally well will appeal to you enough to cause a change in habit.

If you are in the habit of calling your broker or waiting for the daily newspaper to see how the stock market is going, you might not find the allure of an updated-only-fifteen-minutes-ago stock price worth turning on your computer. In some areas, personal computers might offer more power than you'll ever need — and in other areas, they may offer much less.

I wish I could give the rather pat advice, "Try before you buy." Unfortunately, personal computing is rather like flying a plane or visiting Europe or sailing a boat — you'll never know if *you* will like it unless you try it, and trying it is expensive.

If you're uncertain, continue your investigation. If any of the "drawbacks" in this chapter seem like sound, logical, clear-headed arguments for not buying a personal computer, then you probably shouldn't get one — yet. If these drawbacks seem like intolerable nit-picking that no reasonable person would consider for more than a few moments at most, then you're ready.

How long that readiness will last is anybody's guess, and if you guess wrong, it could be a costly error.

You can minimize the chances of disappointment by lowering your expectations. Personal computers do many things well, many things not-so-well, and a broad spectrum of things somewhere between "well" and "not-so-well."

Don't expect a personal computer to change your life, unless you are a professional writer who already knows how to use a typewriter; a small businessperson who has fairly standard small business needs (word processing, accounts receivable, accounts payable, etc.); or someone who devotes a large portion of their time doing something personal computers do well (electronic spreadsheeting, stock marketing, cross-index filing, and the like).

If you don't fall into one of those three categories, it might be best if you lower your expectations to a workable minimum. By "workable minimum" I mean, don't lower them so much that you don't get the computer, but lower them enough so that disappointment will not be one of your peripherals.

Be realistic. Don't expect too much from your computer.

Another way to help insure that you'll use your personal computer more often than your Norman Rockwell Thanksgiving Turkey Platter is to choose carefully. As much as possible, select the computer and programs that meet your current needs and fit comfortably into your lifestyle.

If you want to play computer games, buy the best game-playing computer you can afford — and make sure you like the games that are available for it.

If you are running a small business, there is no need to buy a computer and software designed for a ten-million dollar corporation. (Yes, the salesperson might say, you can grow into it. When you're grossing ten million, however, you can *buy* into it.) If you get more program than you need, you'll have to learn about the complexities of a program that you might use only 25% of, and those complexities besides being expensive — might one day cause the computer to be turned off for good.

If you're just curious about computers and want to get your feet wet, a fish pond will do — there's no need to install an Olympic-sized pool.

As pointed out before, however, if you need word processing, plan on spending enough for a decent personal computer, a letter quality printer, and the best word processing program you can find. The same is true of business: buying too much computer can be a bother; buying too little, disastrous.

There's a quote about suiting the action to the word and the word to the action, but we've already quoted once from *Hamlet* in this book, and one profound Shakespearean reference per computer book is sufficient, I think.

2. Computers are powerful and, therefore, capable of powerful mistakes. It is hard to duplicate, using ordinary methods, the efficiency and effectiveness of a computer. It is equally hard to duplicate, using ordinary methods, the degree of devastation and disaster possible on a computer — unless you consider fire, flood, and nuclear fission "ordinary methods."

Let's assume, for example, that you run a company and have all of your accounting information on a single hard disk. A hard disk is a platter of metal, usually aluminum, spinning at something like 1,800 revolutions per minute, which is equal to 30 revolutions per second. Pretty fast. Let's say that one day, the hard disk decided it was tired of being a hard disk and wanted to become a frisbee.

The disk exercises a remarkable amount of free will for a disk, releases itself from its normally secure housing, and flies out the window, landing in the *Guiness Book of World Records* for The Greatest Distance Traveled by a Personal Computer Hard Disk.

Television news crews are dispatched to interview your disk, while Tom Brokaw and Roger Mudd argue over which one of them will handle the story. (Neither one wants to, but they hear that Dan Rather is opening his broadcast with it, so they feel *somebody* has to interview the damn thing, Tom Snyder and Rona Barrett having both refused.) Roone Arledge can't decide if the story should be on *The ABC Evening News* or *ABC Wide World of Sports*. He decides both.

The MacNeil Lehrer Report cancels its planned satellite interview with Fidel Castro and devotes a special, expanded 90-minute version of the show to your disk.

Also at PBS, both William F. Buckley, Jr. and Dick Cavett are trying to get the disk on their respective shows. "The disk is a celebrity, not a politician," says Cavett. "It belongs on my show."

"The disk is a projectile, and therefore belongs on *Firing Line*," counters Buckley.

In a ceremony on the White House Lawn, your former hard disk is made an honorary frisbee. "This is one small step for disk," the hard disk says as you flip off your TV and mutter something about ungrateful hardware. You try to figure out a way to recover months of priceless financial data, and decide there is no way.

A company once, in a less colorful way, lost all of its accounts receivable information. The company sent out polite form letters asking how much money, if any, each customer owed. Not surprisingly, the company was soon out of business.

Businessman, upon being informed that his hard disk had been turned into a frisbee.

Even a single floppy disk, holding 170 pages of information, can be a tragic loss. The entire text of this book fits comfortably on three 5¼-inch floppy disks. If I were to lose one of these prior to the publication of the book, and I had failed to make back-up copies (which I almost always fail to do), it would surely go beyond tragedy and deep into soap opera. O, the gnashing of teeth and the pulling of hair. Cecil B. DeMille never directed *angst* on a grander scale than I would emote.

There are two possible causes for such unthinkable, but possible, occurrences: computer error and operator error. As much as I hate to admit it, the latter far exceeds the former. By "computer error," I mean both hardware and software. Once again, the latter is the cause of far more difficulty than the former.

The causes of costly mistakes, in order, are:

A. Operator error.

B. Software error.

C. Computer error.

Using software that's been around for a while and a computer that's a relative newcomer, the last two categories might trade places. Almost without a doubt, though, operator error will be responsible for more "computer errors" than anything else.

Suggestions for minimizing this drawback are:

First, make sure you know what you're doing. It's fine to experiment with a computer — there is almost nothing you can do from the keyboard of a personal computer that will cause any permanent damage to the machine — but don't experiment while you're working on something important or irreplaceable.

Before trying anything new, try a test first, or *at least* save whatever is in memory on a diskette. If, for any reason, the computer "crashes," (shuts down, freezes up, or turns off), whatever was in the memory is lost. If it is put on a disk (a simple, swift procedure), then the chance of retrieving the information is greatly enhanced.

Second, buy quality, time-tested software. This may not always be possible. You may need a program that is one-of-a-kind and newly introduced. In that case, watch for bugs and be very careful. If you are using the program to process information that is important to you, call the software manufacturer periodically and ask if any bugs have been reported that you should be aware of.

On the whole, however, most of the major categories

of software — word processing, spell-checking, accounting, electronic spreadsheeting, filing — have products in each category that have been around at least a year, have sold thousands of copies, and have had most of the bugs removed.

Third, take good care of your machine. It doesn't require much. It is estimated that the majority of electronic parts that do not fail within the first twelve months will last for 500 years. How they make such calculations — the transistor being less than thirty years old and the silicon chip less than twenty — I shall never know.

It's a comfort, though, to think that, unless Life Extension Science takes the same dramatic leaps as Computer Science, and soon, our personal computers will be giving pleasure to generations yet unborn. Well, maybe it won't last *that* long, but a computer should hold up until you buy your next computer.

The only parts of the computer that need periodic servicing and attention are the moving parts, and then only the disk drive and the printer. (A good keyboard seems to go on forever, and a joystick, well, use it for twenty years and buy a new one.)

Disk drives should be cleaned periodically. It takes about two minutes: all you do is put a special head-cleaning disk in the drive and turn on the computer. Most "read/ write" (disk) errors are caused by dirty heads, which two minutes of cleaning would have prevented.

Even if the computer misbehaves totally and eats a disk, the failure of the operator to make a back-up disk — again, about a two-minute procedure — can cause the problem to be much larger than necessary.

Power failures, too, cause the computer to lose its memory. Power failures happen with varying degrees of frequency in various locales. While living in Detroit, I don't recall any, except during electrical storms. In New York there were only two, although they lasted several days each. In Los Angeles, the power company named in honor of Mr. Edison seems to fail, on the average, once every other month.

Murphy's Law #253A states, "The power will fail

only when you are about to find out 'whodunit' in a television mystery, have a souffle in the electric oven, or put something irreplaceable into the memory of your computer and have been too lazy to save it on a disk." Law #253B reads, "This will only happen when you are dangerously behind schedule, exhausted, and in a bad mood."

A good slogan to adopt while working with a computer is that of the compulsive bargain shopper: "Save, save, save." I am very bad at this sort of thing, but I do make it a habit to save whatever I am working on whenever I get up. Given that I get up at least every fifteen minutes, it's a rather good plan. Other people less antsy than I might want to save at the end of every page, or every ten minutes (set a timer), or at some predetermined interval or place in their work.

3. Eyestrain. Some people find that peering into a video screen causes eyestrain, and some do not. For those who do, here are some suggestions.

First, try using a monochrome video display rather than color. The images on color screens are not as sharp as images on monochrome screens. The fuzziness might be causing the problem.

Second, a monitor (a video display that plugs directly into the computer, rather than a recycled TV set) gives a sharper image.

Again, fuzziness may be the problem. (When a screen display is fuzzy, the eyes strain to sharpen the focus. This constant straining can cause headaches.)

Third, green phosphor is supposed to be easier on the eyes than white. Try a green phosphor screen for a while.

Fourth, the glare of room lights off the glass of the video screen can cause eyestrain. Get a filter (Polaroid makes a good one) that reduces the reflected light. (The Polaroid filter also improves the contrast of the characters on the video screen, making them easier to read and further reducing eyestrain.)

Fifth, try a "slow phosphor" video display. The image on a video screen changes thirty times per second. This rapid changing is what gives the illusion of motion when

Laverne hits Shirley in the face with a pie or a pizza or something. Ordinary video screens are designed to display the one-thirtieth-of-a-second-image, and then to fade quickly to make way for the next flash.

Slow phosphor holds the image for a longer period of time. Before the last image fades, another has already taken its place, and before that one fades, another has taken its place, and so on. This delivers a video display that is rock-steady.

The disadvantage of slow phosphor is that, because it holds onto a light image so long, when you change something on the screen, "ghosts" of what were formerly there will momentarily remain. These poltergeists remain for less than a second, but for someone used to quick-fade phosphor, it can be annoying. It is, however, far less annoying than eyestrain.

Sixth, read the solutions to disadvantages 4 and 5 below.

Eyestrain does not affect the vast majority of people who use video screens. These suggestions were offered for those who do have trouble.

4. Neck and back strain. Most back and neck strain experienced in front of a personal computer comes from maintaining the same posture, hour after hour.

If the keyboard and video display are all in one piece, your options for shifting positions are limited. You must reach the keys which, attached as they are to the screen, are not easily moved. This makes varying your position difficult. Not surprisingly, this sameness of position is a pain in the neck, a pain in the back, and a pain in any other portion of your anatomy you care to name.

The solution is a simple one: a detachable keyboard. A detachable keyboard allows you to place the video screen where it's most comfortable for viewing, and the keyboard where it's most comfortable for typing.

We have grown accustomed to looking *down* at a page when we type. This is because those of us who learned typing on a typewriter found that, invariably, that's where the paper was. The paper was where the typing was, and that's what we wanted to see.

Video screens can be placed a bit higher — closer to eye-level — and not having to look down for hours at a time can, in terms of neck and back strain, make quite a difference.

Also, the video screen need not be as close as the keyboard. As I write this, the video screen is at least four feet away. To read the entire screen, I only have to move my *eyes*, not my head. (The closer I get to the screen, the more my head would have to move — some law of physics at work there, no doubt.) This causes less strain on my neck and back. Further, the field of my vision encompassed by the video screen is small compared to the amount that would be involved if I were up close. I don't know if it's true or not, but my mother always told me it was bad for my eyes to sit too near the TV screen.

I will, mom's advice notwithstanding, move closer to the video screen when I edit this piece. I will be looking at the text in a critical character-by-character way. Now I'm just looking at words, sentences, and ideas. For those, four feet is close enough.

But even when I move up close, I will never be as close as I would have to be if the keyboard were permanently glued to some spot directly under the video screen.

A detachable keyboard also allows for an infinite variety of positions. Some of this chapter I have written with the keyboard on my desk, some of it with the keyboard on my lap. Were I so inclined, I could have stood up, lain down, or assumed any of a dozen other positions.

Maybe it's true that the straight-backed rigid posture is the best for long-term typing, but I never learned to sit like that, and I doubt if I ever will. There is too much else to learn before and after getting a computer. Who wants to have to worry about learning a new way to *sit?*

I would rather have a computer that adapts its shape to my posture, not one that demands I adapt my posture to its shape, especially when that shape is dictated by an 1874 invention. Personal computers with attached keyboards were modeled after computer terminals, and computer terminals were modeled after typewriters. This was because computer terminals were designed for secretaries who were already familiar with typewriters.

Besides, if there's any validity to the next point, the further away the video screen, the better I feel.

5. Radiation. *All* TV screens, including the one in your bedroom and the one in your living room, give off radiation. The electron gun shoots electrons, "radiating" the phosphor until it glows. Some of this radiation leaks out.

How much leaks out is not known. How much is safe to be exposed to is not known. What the effects of this are over time are not known.

"But how can you be sure there's no danger from radiation?"

A few things are known:

A. The farther you are from the video screen the less radiation you are exposed to. Radiation levels drop quickly with distance. A few inches from a video screen, a measurable amount of radiation is given off; several feet away, the amount is no longer measurable.

B. Color monitors give off more radiation — as much as five times more — than monochrome.

C. Radiation is not good for you.

I remember looking at a sign in front of a building on my first trip to Los Angeles in the early 1970s. It said,

"UCLA CENTER FOR UNCLEAR MEDICINE."

I thought, only in Southern California would a medical center admit that there were any areas of medicine that were unclear; and to put it on a sign, and to devote a whole center to it — well, I was impressed.

A friend had to point out to me that the sign read UCLA CENTER FOR NUCLEAR MEDICINE. Since that time, I have been unable to look at the word NUCLEAR without seeing the word UNCLEAR.

The reports that have surfaced over the past ten years have only made it more unclear. Atomic bombs, meltdowns, nuclear energy, annihilation — did this perplexing subject have to pop out of Pandora's Box *on television*, too? Do we have to face major moral, social, and medical issues every time we turn on the TV or switch on the computer? I mean, can't they leave us *SCTV* and Space Invaders? Is nothing sacred?

A polling of the scientific community only heightens the dilemma. Some say radiation from video screens causes cataracts, miscarriages, leukemia, and arthritis, especially in the fingers because, on computers without detachable keyboards, the fingers are closest to the video screen for the longest periods of time.

"But I can't see any radiation."

Other scientists say that the chance a radioactive electron has of passing through the glass of a video screen is about the chance you or I would have of driving through Nevada with four feet of beachballs on the ground and a gallon of gas in the car. (I did not make that up. A nuclear scientist made that up. A man with credentials.) They say that even the sun gives off radioactivity, and that there is as much danger being exposed to daylight as there is to video light.

The more intricate the arguments, the more persuasive each side became. The only advice I could offer concerned computer users: use a monochrome video screen, and put it as far away from you as possible. (Yet another argument for the detachable keyboard.)

But then I wondered: should I be giving this advice at all? Maybe there's no danger to begin with. What's the point in scaring people? *The China Syndrome* was bad enough. No point in starting *The Computa Syndrome.* I was in the midst of deepening confusion when, suddenly, a solution appeared.

The Langley-St. Clair Company began marketing lead-impregnated acrylic screens that fit over regular video screens and block, according to Langley-St.Clair, 100% of all x-rays and most ultraviolet radiation. The acrylic, it turns out, was originally designed for windows in nuclear power plants.

I ordered one. It arrived, a sturdy piece of plastic, about a quarter of an inch thick; transparent, with a slight tint. It attached easily to my video screen with velcro tape. I felt safe from radiation, like Lex Luthor felt safe from Superman when wearing his Kryptonite-impregnated leisure suit. It was the magic shield of Gardol from my youth.

The only problem is that the acrylic screen reflects light almost like a mirror. Who wants to trade safety for annoying glare? (It's trade-off time again.) The Langley-St. Clair people readily admit the problem and, by the time you read this, they should have it solved. They plan to cover their acrylic with the Polaroid anti-glare screen mentioned earlier in the chapter. The whole package should cost around $100. (If they don't have it, their regular screen is about $50 and Polaroid's is around $70.) Not a bad price for no glare, improved video screen contrast, and peace of mind.

Well, those are all the drawbacks I've discovered about personal computers, except for unknowledgeable salespeople, lack of product support, and manufacturers arrogance and incompetence. But I'll discuss those in the chapters ahead. Besides, I never let those things stop me from having something I want. If I did, I wouldn't have a telephone.

A Periodic Table

#	Symbol	Label
1	G	GLUE
2	S	SPIDERS
3	Tu	TUBAS
4	R	RAIN
5	L	LUCK
6	Sp	SPRINGS
7	T	TODAY
8	Ci	CIRCLES
9	P	PLAY MONEY
10	C	COTTON
11	E	ELBOWS
12	F	FISH
13	J	JOGGERS
14	D	DIRT
15	W	WRONG
16	H	HONEY
17	M	MONEY
18	F	FACES
19	W	WINKS
20	Mu	MUD
21	Pd	PUDDLES
22	Ju	JUSTICE
23	Ck	CRACKERS
24	Rt	RITA
25	Rc	PHOTOS
26	Jo	JOE
27	Yo	YOU
28	Me	ME
29	Y	YELLOW
30	Da	DACRON
31	Ri	RICE
32	Ic	ICONS
33	An	ANIMALS
34	I	INK
35	Pa	PASTE
36	Cr	CROUTONS
37	Bg	PLUMS
38	Wh	WEALTH
39	Ev	EVIL
40	Cn	CARTONS
41	Li	LIPS
42	Po	POOLS
43	U	UNDERWEAR
44	Cy	CRAYONS
45	Dg	DOGS
46	Mr	MARS
47	N	NATO
48	Ru	RUGS
49	Go	GOODIES
50	Mt	MEAT
51	Fe	FEAR
52	Tv	TVS
53	Fb	FLUG BUGS
54	Ca	CARS
55	Ld	LADLES
56	Gu	GNUS
57	Lt	CANADA
58	Cc	COCO
59	Im	IMPS
60	Er	ERROR
61	V	VACUUM
62	Bc	BIG CATS
63	Ct	CATS
64	Tu	TRUST
65	Cu	CRUD
66	Se	SEX
67	Lc	THE DOG
68	Sh	SHOES
69	Id	IDEAS
70	Mk	MONKEYS
71	De	DEATH
72	To	TOGAS
73	So	SOAP
74	Le	LEMONS
75	Lv	LOVE
76	Ta	TAPE
77	Tk	TALK
78	Eg	EGG NOG
79	Co	CONCRETE
80	Go	GOODIES
81	Lf	LIFE
82	Go	GOODIES
83	Sc	SCORPIO
84	Ar	ART
85	Ha	HAWAII
86	Sl	STEALTH
87	Us	US
88	Th	THEM
89	Cd	CANADA
90	Fg	FIRST GRADE
91	Wb	WATER BALLOONS
92	Ly	LUCY
93	Sy	STANLEY
94	Hi	HICCUPS
95	Fd	FIDO
96	Cg	CIGARS
97	Lg	LUGNUTS
98	Ff	FOO-FOO
99	Cw	COW
100	Gm	GUM
101	Mn	MOON
102	Su	SUN
103	Fr	FROST

You can use T.K. Atherton's handy Periodic Table in selecting your personal computer.

Selecting a Personal Computer

Whenever I hear the words "selecting" or "choosing," I am reminded of a piece I read in *Daily Variety*. "Johnny Mathis 'coptered to his Irvine Meadows concert, but when the chopper refused to start-up after the show, Mathis chose to be driven home by car to L.A."

He *chose* to be driven home by car to L.A.? What, do you suppose, were his other choices? Riding a bicycle? Hitchhiking? Moving to Irvine Meadows?

If you are in the market for a personal computer and you only have $100 to spend, your choices are about as narrow as Mr. Mathis's. If you have $300-$400 to spend, your choices broaden. If you have several thousand to spend — or, rather, invest — the selection, and selecting, can be almost staggering.

My first piece of advice is, don't take it all that seriously. If you buy a personal computer now, and you like it, chances are* you'll be buying another one within the next few years. Most gourmet cooks are on their second or third Cuisinart. You may not like hearing this, just as car buyers in the early 1900s on the verge of buying their first car would not like to have been told that they would own ten or fifteen more cars during their lifetimes...but most of them did.

Still, you should choose your first personal computer carefully. Your first experiences with your first computer will invariably color your views of personal computers and computing for some time.

There are three factors to be considered when buying a personal computer:

1. What you want to use the computer for.
2. How quickly you want to do that on a computer.
3. Your budget.

Let's look at each of these points individually.

---

*One of my favorite songs, Johnny. Honest.

1. What you want to use the computer for. Although it's the program that determines what a personal computer does, certain personal computers run some programs better than others.

Personal computers fall roughly into two camps: those that process and display characters (letters and numbers) well, and those that process and display color graphics (spaceships and bar graphs) well. In general, the two are mutually exclusive.

One reason is the processor. Most processors in most personal computers are either designed — or at least utilized within the computer — to process either graphics or characters. This limitation is true of the current marketplace and will not be true a few years from now. The IBM Personal Computer, for example, is equally adept at handling either color graphics or characters.

Another reason is the limitation of the color video monitor. Color monitors, even the best, do not display letters and numbers as sharply as monochrome monitors do. This is likely to remain true for some time. Heaven knows millions of dollars have been spent on sharpening the image of color TV screens and no one — remembering the round, fuzzy pictures from the first color televisions — can deny that vast improvements have been made. It remains true, however, that even after these many millions invested and vast improvements made, the monochrome display is still sharper than the color.

Not that you can't process words and numbers on a color screen, or play graphic games on a monochrome screen — you can — but you will be happier, in the long run, processing characters on a personal computer designed for characters and processing graphics on a computer designed for graphics.

This division in personal computer design comes from the same two camps that nurture personal computers today: home and business.

The personal computer in the home is basically an entertainment device. Several personal computers can trace their ancestry back to the crude video games of the early 1970s. (Remember PONG?) They grew into computers aimed at the average American consumer, and this usually meant careful attention to color graphics. Even when characters were later added, the characters had to be in color. (Most people had just gotten color TV. *Nobody* wanted to go back to black & white.)

The personal computer in business is an ongoing miniaturization of the monoliths of the 1950s. It was a major breakthrough in business computers when a company no longer needed a climatically-controlled computer room. By the time a business computer was small enough to fit into an ordinary *closet*, well, that was something. To a business, the mere fact that data could be displayed on a *screen* — any screen — and not require a teletypewriter printout, was more than enough. Color? Who needs color? When the color green came to office video screens, that was plenty.

So the home/hobbyist computer continued to grow, and the mainframe/business computer continued to shrink, and today they're both getting close to the same size, and that size is recognizable as the personal computer.

It's an eventful time, rather like the driving of the golden spike that connected the railroads of the East and West. Like the Transcontinental Railroad, one group of computer manufacturers began (the home/hobbyist group) in the West and another group of computer manufacturers (the mainframe/business group) began in the East, and they're coming together in terms of size and philosophy somewhere out there in the Midwest, each hoping to capture the heartland of America.

There's no *reason* it started on both coasts and moved in. It could have, like broadcasting, started in the middle and moved out. (Network radio started in Chicago, and eventually moved to New York and L.A.) But moving in it is, and if you're going to be selecting a personal computer in the next, say, year — prior to the Japanese invasion (known affectionately among American computer manufacturers as "Pearl Harbor II") — it's good to keep these origins, and their differences, in mind.

So, if you want to use your personal computer to play graphic games, balance your checkbook in full color, and teach a young child the alphabet, you are in luck — there are several fine computers that do all of these well.

Or, if you want a computer for word processing, accounting, and displaying up-to-the-fifteen-minutes-ago stock market prices, you, too, are in luck — there are many fine computers that do these things as well.

If, however, you want to play full-color graphic games *and* process words, or do full-scale accounting *and* teach a young child the alphabet, you will have to select your computer more carefully and either (a) make compromises, or (b) spend more money.

2. How quickly do you want to do that on a computer? The world of personal computing is changing so rapidly that, every day you wait, the personal computer you eventually buy will do more and/or cost less.

This has always been true of technology. Light bulbs, when they were first introduced, cost a dollar. That was back in the days when people were making about ten cents an hour. Although light bulbs are a dollar again, people make more than ten cents an hour.

It's how badly you want the new technology, and how much it will do for you, that determines if you should buy now or save later.

In 1975, I bought one of the first video recorders offered for the home market, a Betamax. Each tape recorded for an hour. The timer turned the machine on and off, once, in any 24-hour period. It cost about $1,000.

In 1976, I bought a Betamax II. This recorded for two hours, allowing me to record entire movies while away from home. The timer, still, turned on and off once during any 24-hour cycle. It cost about $1,000.

In 1980, I bought a Betamax III. It recorded for up to five hours. I could set the timer to record four different programs on four different channels over a fourteen-day period. It had a remote control switch that allowed for fast forward (no more commercials), rewind (instant replays), slow motion, and freeze frame. It cost about $1,000.

Were I to buy a video player today, I could have all of the above features, plus eight hours of recording time, wireless remote control, and portability. What would it cost me? Oh, about $1,000.

And so it has been and will continue to be with personal computers. If someone were to ask me about my early purchase of a video recorder, "Don't you wish you would have waited?" I would reply with an unconditional "No." I feel I got a thousand dollars' worth of use out of the first Betamax, and certainly more than a thousand dollars' worth of use out of the second and, thus far, more than a thousand dollars' worth of use out of the third.

But that's me. I use it a lot and enjoy it a lot, and I do not feel that $3,000 for the past seven years' worth of use is unreasonable. I do not, however, feel that I need eight hours of recording, or wireless remote, or portability. Although I'd use them if I had them, they're not worth $1,000 to me. But they might be to someone else. I cannot, just because I happen to love and adore my personal computer, recommend that you run out and buy one. I use mine every day. You might not.

I gave my mother my first two Betamaxes and, in the past seven years, I doubt if she's used them twenty times. I gave her a phone answering machine. It seems to make a nice telephone stand, but it never gets turned on. If I were to give my mother a personal computer, it might be used as a nightlight, but that's about all. My mother has no real need for personal computers. Pizza, yes. Personal computers, no.

My brother, on the other hand is, like me, a writer. He spent three years writing stories on the computer at the newspaper where he worked. Now that he's moved to the Big Apple, he could use a computer to process his words with. (My mother and I bought him one for his birthday.)

If you have a need for a computer, but are waiting for prices to go down, buy the computer now. What you get from the computer as it fills your need will more than balance whatever saving you may gain by waiting. If you don't have a need for a computer, you can get it sooner or later, and it may not make much difference.

3. Your budget. Personal computers are available from $100 to $5,000. That's quite a range, and there are quite a range of features within that range. Which computer to get, or to get a computer at all, will depend on what you have to spend.

For example, a Timex/Sinclair, for $100, will attach to any TV and display words and symbols in black & white. You can, among other things, write and run BASIC programs on it. For $300 you can get a VIC-20, which has a color display, a much better keyboard, and far more adaptability. You get much more computer for $300 but, for many people interested in computing, $100 is already stretching it.

At $3,995, the Victor 9000 is a superb computer: two disk drives, monochrome video screen, detachable keyboard and yet, for $1,795, you can get a terrific computer, the KayPro II: two disk drives, monochrome video screen, and detachable keyboard. For a small business, the Victor 9000 is a bargain. For a struggling writer, the KayPro II is a blessing.

Personal computers, like cars, offer everything from transportation specials to limousines.

Before purchasing a personal computer, many people try to figure out which computer manufacturer will be in business five or ten years from now. These might be the same people who bought a DuMont television back in the early fifties.

I wouldn't spend a great deal of time wondering about that. Nobody knows. Here, for example, are some of the cars that were on the market in 1927: Ajax, Auburn, Buick, Cadillac, Chandler, Chevrolet, Chrysler, Cleveland, Dodge, Durant, Erskine, Essex, Flint, Ford, Gardner, Gray, Hudson, Hupmobile, Jewett, Jordan, La Salle, Locomobile Jr. 8, Maxwell, Moon, Nash, Oakland, Oldsmobile, Overland, Packard, Paige, Peerless, Pontiac, Reo, Rickenbacker, Star, Studebaker, Velie, Willys-Knight, and the ever-popular Whippet-Overland.

Do you think you could have selected one of the eight cars from this list that would still be manufactured 55 years later? And, if you could have, would it have made any difference?

The gold rush is on, and California is again its focal point; only this time it's not Sutter's Mill but Silicon Valley that draws the prospectors. "Computers or Bust!" More than one company has staked its corporate stick on some aspect or other of the microprocessing world. (If this book doesn't make it, *I'm* up a creek, and it's not Sutter's.)

There will be an alarming increase of computers and computer companies, followed by a leveling off, followed by a winnowing out. There will be bankruptcies, buy-outs, and mergers. (Shugart and Radio Shack forming Shugart Shack; Victor, RCA, and Vector forming RCA Victor-Vector; and maybe even Timex/IBM.)

You'll note in the above listing of automobiles the absence of Toyota, Datsun, and Honda. What about the "invasion" of the Japanese? Some people like to think, and voice their thoughts rather loudly, that American superiority in the field of computers is unsurpassable — even though more than half the printers sold in this country are made in Japan, as are a goodly percentage of the microprocessors, transistors, and other electronic innards of "American Made" personal computers.

Besides, The Big Three computermakers are acting more like The Big Three automakers every day.

Apple is using Ford's plan to advertise away all problems. The Apple II and Apple III are, dollar-for-dollar, not very good values. However, Apple's advertising campaign would have you believe you are paying a bit extra for *quality*. (Ford: "Quality is Job #1.") The fact is that, with the Apple II, you are paying for a computer design that is six years old — ancient by personal computer standards — and, of course, the ads necessary to keep it selling. Apple is planning, I hear, to introduce a new line of personal computers. They should have come out years ago.

Atari is like Chrysler. A good chunk of Chrysler's income comes from repackaging and marketing Japanese imports. A good chunk of Atari's income comes from repackaging and marketing one Japanese import in particular, Pac-Man.

Like General Motors, Radio Shack is the more conservative and financially secure of the three. On the whole, however, a Radio Shack computer is about as interesting as a Chevrolet. They both sell well, but so what? One day, right in the middle of *Good Morning America*, the consumers of this country will wake up and yawn, and that will be the end of GM and TRS.

Commodore has found a good thing in the VIC-20, and American Motors has found a good thing in the Renault, and they're both running with it. Beyond that, I don't know what either one of them is doing. I find their confusing array of cars and computers incomprehensible.

Maybe ironically, and maybe not, it's old Big Blue, ultra-conservative IBM — so slow to respond to a rapidly changing marketplace that they've been the butt of jokes around small computer circles for years — who seem to be offering the only real and dynamic challenge to foreign competition in the personal computer market.

They started from scratch, and using sound research and engineering principles, built a fine computer. They are marketing it in an aggressive yet intelligent way, with advertising that is attractive, informative, and understated.

I do not own stock in IBM; I do not even own an IBM. In fact, I sold my IBM (Selectric) to buy my personal computer. If you would have told me two years ago that I would be writing good things about IBM, I would have told you you were crazy. IBM has always represented to me the worst aspects of Big Business. Now I only have AT&T to dislike.

I have simply been watching, with a cool and dispassionate eye, the way IBM introduced and has supported their Personal Computer, and I am impressed. Unfortunately, we do not have an American auto company that parallels IBM.

So, don't pick a computer based upon how long you think the company might last. The list of computers changes monthly — certainly yearly — and ten years from now we will all laugh at the funny-sounding computer names, and the old timers among us will tell tales of how they once knew somebody who actually owned one.

And expect the Japanese to be here soon, in great numbers, offering the same quality at low prices that they have already brought to automobiles, electronics, cameras, and even steel.

Let's look at the basic component parts of the personal computer from a buyer's point of view.

Microprocessor

There are basically two types of microprocessors in personal computers today: **8-bit** and **16-bit**. Most personal computers are of the 8-bit variety, although an increasing number of 16-bit machines are being introduced.

Sixteen-bit microprocessors are more powerful than eight-bit, and more than just twice as powerful.

To illustrate, imagine a calculator that was capable of displaying eight columns of binary numbers. (See *Chapter Two*.) The value of the column at the far left would be 128. If, however, the calculator were extended to include 16 columns, the value of the far-left column would be 32,768. I don't know if there's a technical term that compares the relationship between the number 128 and .32,768. A non-technical term would be "significant."

Although this isn't exactly what goes on inside of a microprocessor, the example is given to illustrate that 16, in the world of computers, can be more powerful than "twice eight."

The use of 16-bit microprocessors is still in its infancy, and the potential they offer has yet to be tapped. Most software available for them is simply quickly re-written versions of 8-bit programs.

For the present, the major benefit of 16-bit computers is that the user-programmable memory can be increased. The maximum amount of user-programmable memory (RAM) an 8-bit machine can handle is 64K. For some programs, the ability to access 128K or 256K of memory is desirable, but unfortunately, not possible on an 8-bit machine. With a 16-bit machine, it is.

The fact that there is so little software available for 16-bit machines has prompted peripheral manufacturers to come out with plug-in cards that turn 16-bit machines back into 8-bit machines. This is rather like the phonographs back in the fifties that played both 78s and 33s.

For the present, an 8-bit personal computer is more than sufficient for almost all computing applications. In fact, many people buy 16-bit machines (the IBM Personal Computer and Victor 9000, for example) because they like the screen or the keyboard, not the microprocessor. Since the personal computing world is more comfortable with 8-bit computers, more than one person has told me of the IBM and Victor, "I wish this were an 8-bit machine."

For 8-bit machines used for the display and processing of words and numbers, the most popular microprocessor is the Z-80. The Z-80 allows the use of CP/M, the most popular operating system for non-game computers.

Operating Systems

While we're on the subject of CP/M, we might as well discuss operating systems. "Operating system" is a shortened version of **Disk Operating System**, also known as **DOS**.

A disk operating system simply tells the computer how to store information on the disk, and how to retrieve stored information from the disk. For the most part, the operating system is transparent to the user. The user is involved with running a specific program, and the computer runs the DOS to let it know how to interact with the disk drives.

If you take the computer-is-like-the-phonograph-and-the-program-is-like-the-record analogy from an earlier chapter, you can look at the operating system as the *kind* of record being played (78, 45, 33), and the specific program (word processing, accounting, spreadsheeting) as the *contents* of the record (Beethoven, Bowie, Draper).

It is only important to know about record formats when you buy a phonograph and when you buy recordings. To purchase a phonograph that only plays 78s might have been a good investment forty years ago, but it wouldn't make much sense today. Almost all records are either 33s or 45s, and you purchase a phonograph accordingly. When you're actually playing a song, it's impossible to tell if it's coming from a 45 or a 33.

The disk operating system on a computer is very much the same way. Once you are running a program, you would be hard-pressed to tell which operating system you were using.

However, the choice of operating system for personal computers is far more complicated than the choice of which phonograph to buy. In terms of operating systems for 8-bit machines, there's CP/M, and then there's everything else.

Apple has its own operating system. Radio Shack has its own operating system. Commodore has its own operating system. And so on. Selecting an operating system is not like choosing between 78s and 33s; it's like choosing between records, cassettes, 8-tracks, video disks, video tapes, microcassettes, and all the other possible methods of playing back recordings.

For some, the choice is made because of the programs available in a specific format. If you like the software offered for Apple, you must get the Apple operating system. The programs in TRSDOS (Tandy Radio Shack Disk Operating System) will not run on anything but a machine operating under TRSDOS.

For others, the choice will be based upon the machine. If you really *like* Commodore, then you use the Commodore operating system and choose your programs from the library of Commodore software.

For business, the choice is usually CP/M. A great many machines run CP/M, and the CP/M library is vast. CP/M, however, is not good at the graphic games many people want their personal computers to play. For most business applications, though, you'll find CP/M your best choice.

Then there are the 16-bit machines. There are only two major operating systems for 16-bit machines, IBMDOS and CP/M-86. CP/M-86 is the 16-bit version of CP/M. IBMDOS is IBM's disk operating system. Both are (of course) incompatible, so the race is on. IBM seems to be winning, simply because it's selling more 16-bit computers than anyone else, and every IBM comes with IBMDOS. (The Victor people are not taking sides: each Victor 9000 comes with both CP/M-86 *and* IBMDOS.)

It's an unfortunate situation. If you want the games of Atari and Apple, you'll have to buy an Atari *and* an Apple. It's rather like RCA selling records that will only play on RCA phonographs and Columbia is selling records that will only play on Columbia phonographs.

Disk Drives

Disks come in two sizes: 5¼-inch and 8-inch. (Although Sony is beginning to market a 3½-inch disk. Stay tuned. Film at eleven.)

5¼-inch drives are the most popular in the world of personal computing. They're more compact and easier to handle. A 5¼-inch disk can hold from 72K to 640K of information, depending on the computer. (K stands for kilobyte, or 1,024 characters. A double-spaced, typewritten page holds about 2K. To roughly figure disk capacity in pages, divide the number of K by two. 72K equals approximately 36 pages, 640K equals about 320 pages, and so on.)

The amount of disk capacity you'll need will depend upon the kind of programs you'll be running. Some programs, such as accounting, require large disk capacity, and may necessitate a hard disk. For most other business applications, 150K per drive should be considered a minimum.

The question then arises: Should I get one disk drive or two? For almost any business application, two is necessary. The need to make back-up copies of disks is crucial and, although copies of disks can be made on one-drive machines, it's much easier and faster with two drives.

For home use — storing BASIC programs and playing games — one drive of about 100K should suffice. Drives cost upwards of $300, and most homes could find better places to spend the cost of a second drive. One disk drive is recommended, however. Cassette tapes as a medium for storing computer information are slow, limited, and prone to error. Disks, by comparison, are fast, sure, and reliable.

Now, are you ready for some more confusion? Almost every manufacturer of personal computers has its own *format* for storing information on disks. This is not the same as the disk operating system, which tells the computer how to get at that information. The disk format is the way the information is stored physically on the disk by the disk drive. (I warned you it got more confusing.)

Returning to our phonograph analogy (talk about wearing out a record), let's say that the disk operating systems were 78s, 33s, and 45s. One record manufacturer may, for example, start the groove near the spindle, so that records play from the inside out. Another manufacturer may start the groove in the middle, play to the end, then pick up the arm, go to the beginning, and play to the middle.

And so it is with disk formats: everybody's got a different one. So, even if a program were written onto a disk using the CP/M disk operating system, it would probably not be compatible with any other computer, even if that computer were designed to run CP/M. A disk made in a NorthStar Advantage could not run on a TeleVideo 802 or a KayPro II or a Heath-89 — even though all four machines use 5¼-inch disks and can run CP/M.

Why this floppy disk Tower of Babel I will never know. There has been some talk about finding a standard for 5¼-inch disks, although it hasn't gotten very far. There is a standard for 8-inch disks, however — the IBM standard. (IBM invented floppy disks, but were, at the time, primarily interested in the 8-inch format. The 5¼-inch format fell into the hands of several microcomputer manufacturers simultaneously, and they each developed incompatible systems. Maybe it's all continuing today out of some sense of *tradition*.)

There are ways of transferring disks from one machine's format to another, providing that they are written in the same operating system. This can be done by some computer stores and costs about $20 per disk.

Keyboards

Membrane keyboards should be eliminated unless (a) money is tight or (b) you almost never plan to use the keyboard. On an Atari 400, for example, if you're using joysticks and playing games most of the time, you might never touch the keyboard except to answer the question, "Do you want to play again?" To push an occasional "Y" or "N" does not require an elaborate keyboard.

If, however, you want to do programming, typing, budgeting, or any other tasks requiring more than a flirting pass at the keyboard, avoid membrane keyboards.

When we examine keyboards that have movable keys, we find two different kinds: the cheaper-feeling keyboards

An Apple II keyboard

A TeleVideo 802 keyboard

and the more expensive-feeling keyboards. Cheaper keyboards feel, well, cheap. You get the sense that the keyboard design was not of primary concern to the designers of the computer, and it's clear that no one walked around saying, "Cost is no object!" when it came time to manufacture.

Other computer keyboards have a firm, solid feel to them. They were obviously designed for people who would spend a great deal of time working at a keyboard — writers, secretaries, accountants. You'll see what I mean when you compare the keyboards of, say, an Apple II with a KayPro II, or a Radio Shack III with a TeleVideo 802.

If you do little with your keyboard — use it to communicate with a data bank or record personal bank balances — the keyboard is not a major concern. If you plan to do some work at your keyboard — writing, accounting, even programming — select your keyboard as you would a spouse: you'll be spending a lot of intimate time together.

If you plan to do accounting on a personal computer, a numeric keypad is a must. This is a square of keys to the right of the regular keyboard that allows one to enter numbers quickly and easily.

Video Display
Personal computers use two kinds of video display: **monitors** and **TV sets**.

Some computers use a device known as an RF generator to broadcast a signal to your TV. This little generator costs about $5. When you consider the millions spent on equipment by TV stations to get a sharp, clear picture into your home, you can imagine the quality of the picture produced for $5. It's OK, but not great.

Monitors, on the other hand, plug directly into the computer. They produce sharper images than do RF-generated TV pictures.

Be careful when you look at computers that use your TV set for the picture display. Often these computers are demonstrated using color monitors, not ordinary TV sets with RF generators. Many people have been disappointed by the images on their TV set once they got the computer home.

Another thing to be aware of is the penny-wise-pound-foolish possibility inherent in using your home TV. It seems logical to assume that, since one already has a TV, one might as well use it for a display. This is true — if you live alone.

What some people fail to consider, however, is that the TV cannot be used for anything else during Computer-time and, contrary to the Atari ads, the entire family will not want to gather around the TV *every night* and play video games. Occasionally, someone's going to want to watch *Happy Days*, and the battle for the control of the set is on.

The typically American four-TV-four-person household need not worry about this. They might, however, worry about the sharpness of the images, and that is another matter.

To play games, images do not have to be sharp. If a spaceship is a little fuzzy or the line of a maze is a little out of focus, people don't seem to notice. It's the action and the color and the movement one is concerned with.

When working with words and numbers, however, the fuzziness on the screen can be annoying.

One may wind up investing in that $300 monochrome or $850 color monitor after all — only to discover that the computer they bought so that they could save money by hooking it up to the TV doesn't produce the greatest letters and numbers anyway.

Some computers display only 40 characters across the screen. This is known as a **40-column screen**. Some produce 65 characters per line (a 65-column screen), while others produce 80 (an 80-column screen). Forty-column screens are OK for, say, reading classified ads on The Source or programming in BASIC, but for any serious letter-writing or accounting, 65 columns should be considered a minimum, and 80 columns are highly recommended.

Some computers, too, do not display uppercase and lowercase characters, just uppercase. Unless one were doing nothing but sending telegrams, any sort of writing on the computer would require both.

As touched on in the previous chapter, monochrome displays are sharper than color displays and are recommended for everything but color games and graphics. It is said that green phosphor is easier on the eyes than black & white.

As T.K. Atherton's drawing illustrates, a personal computer may or may not speed up scientific research/

The McWilliams II
Word Processor

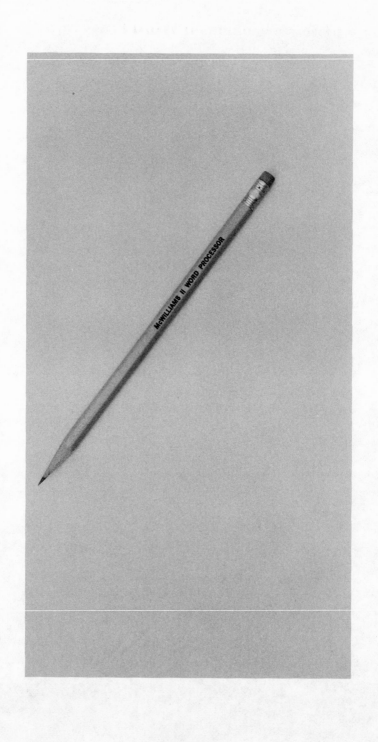

The McWilliams II Word Processor

Features:

- Portable.
- Prints characters from every known language.
- Graphics are fully supported.
- Gives off no appreciable degree of radiation.
- Uses no energy.
- Memory is not lost during a power failure.
- Infinitely variable margins.
- Type sizes from 1 to 945, 257, 256, 256 points.
- Easy to learn.
- User friendly.
- Not likely to be stolen.
- No moving parts.
- Silent operation.
- Occasional maintenance keeps it in top condition.
- Five year unconditional warranty.

Taken from "Questions & Answers on Word Processing."

Preparing the McWilliams II for Action

The **point** of the McWilliams II Word Processor is protected during shipping by a sturdy wooden covering. Before you can use the McWilliams II, you must carefully remove this covering. The McWilliams Computer Corporation sells three (3) instruments designed especially for this purpose:

The George Washington Carver Memorial Sharpener. This precision instrument was named in honor of one of America's greatest botanists, who did remarkable things to peanuts or soybeans or something. Can also be used for chopping vegetables. $25.

The Christopher Columbus Whole World in His Hands Memorial Sharpener: This sharpener honors one of Italy's greatest Americans who, in 1492 sailed the ocean blue to prove that the earth was not flat. He did, and you never need settle for a flat point on your McWilliams II again. $100

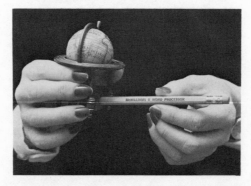

The McWilliams Pro. The ultimate. Electrical energy runs a motor containing ball bearings for the very best point available in word processing today. Fast, precise, exacting. Expensive, but worth it. $500.

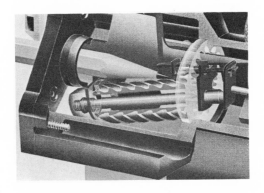

Instructions for Use

(See "The McWilliams Dictionary of Complicated Computer Terms" for words in bold face you might not understand.)

Creating a file: Place a **sheet** of **paper** under **point** of the McWilliams II. Create.

Saving a file: Put the piece of paper in a **safe place.**

Deleting a file: Crumple the piece of paper and **toss** in **waste basket.**

Deleting text: Place **eraser** ("deprocessor") side of the McWilliams II over the portion of the file to be deleted. Rub and rub. Portions of text under the eraser will magically disappear. Brush away magic dust.

Inserting text: Make a **little mark** (^) under the line and between the letters you wish to insert text. Insert text above the line. Use extra **paper** if necessary.

Advanced Features

Electronic mail: Text created with the McWilliams II can be sent over ordinary telephone lines and instantly received in any portion of the world. Follow these simple instructions:

1. Lift receiver off telephone.
2. Dial number of receiving party.
3. Get receiving party on the other end of line.
4. Read receiving party text written by the McWilliams II.

(Note: If receiving party has a McWilliams II, he or she can make a faithful facsimile of your transmission.)

Checkbook Balancing: Use the McWilliams II to record the amount and payee of each check you write, as well as deposits. Add the deposits and subtract the amount of checks written, and in this way the McWilliams II will always keep your check book balanced.

In the kitchen: The McWilliams II can be an invaluable kitchen helper. For example, if your recipe was designed to feed four people, but eight are coming to dinner, you will be glad you have the McWilliams II. Simply use your McWilliams II to *double* all amounts listed in your recipe. One cup becomes two cups, one teaspoon becomes two teaspoons, one egg becomes two eggs, and so on. (Helpful hint: Do *not* double cooking times.)

Peripheral

If you have read in *Time* and *Newsweek* and all those other New York magazines about the Lisa and its mouse, we offer a special mouse peripheral for The McWilliams II. This mouse gives your McWilliams II a **mega delete** option. $275.

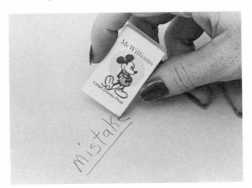

Warranty

Every McWilliams II comes with an unconditional five year guarantee. If anything goes wrong with your McWilliams II, simply return it to us (along with $5 for postage and handling), and we'll be happy to repair it or send you a new one *absolutely free.*

For best results, use only McWilliams Velvacoat Paper.

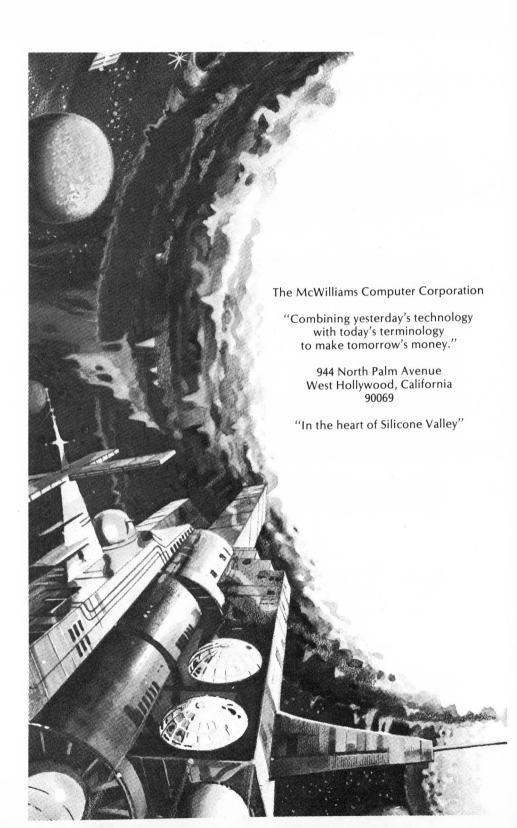

The McWilliams Computer Corporation

"Combining yesterday's technology
with today's terminology
to make tomorrow's money."

944 North Palm Avenue
West Hollywood, California
90069

"In the heart of Silicone Valley"

A Name-Brand Buying Guide

This chapter is incomplete and obsolete. Even as I write, computers are being introduced and improvements being made on personal computers already on the market.

When all makes and models are accounted for, there are something like 200 personal computers on the market. This does not include software, printers, or other peripherals.

To spend just one day with each of these computers would take me the better part of a year, and to devote but one page to each of them would take the better part of this book.

I am reminded of a *Ripley's Believe It or Not* item from my childhood. It said that if the population of China were to line up and march four abreast past a point, the line would never end. Their rate of reproduction was faster than the number of people moving past the point. (I wondered, precocious youngster that I was, how they could reproduce that fast while standing in line.)

Reviewing computers, I fear, would have the same effect. By the time the 200 days were done, there would be another hundred computers to look at, and by the time I got through those, it would be time to start all over with revisions and improvements.

During all the days spent with these machines, of course, this book would not be in your hands. I postponed the publication of **The Word Processing Book** twelve times. Every week I heard about something new, and every week I thought, "I'd better investigate this — it's worth waiting a week if I can include it."

Three months later I had to draw the line: "What I know about word processing *today* will encompass the first edition of the book, and that's that."

And so it is with this book. What I know about personal computers right now is what will be in the book. I have more to learn than ever. Please do not consider me an expert. Think of me as, say, a friend of a friend, and hold my recommendations in that light.

Naturally, this information will change over time. You are welcome to write and ask for periodically issued Updates on personal computers. More about this at the end of the chapter.

Please don't let me, or anyone, select a computer for you. Personal computers are, above all, personal. What one person likes, another person dislikes; what one person finds annoying, another person might not notice. Like buying a car, you'll have to "test drive" a number of computers before you can comfortably decide, "Yes, this is the one for me."

At best, I will place before you a computer or two that you may not have considered before.

One final warning: these "reviews" are subjective and heavily biased. This chapter is nothing but my opinions and, just because they happen to be bound within the pages of a book, gives them no more credibility than any one else's.

An Introduction to the Symbols Used in This Chapter

The International Association of Computer Reviewers and Publishers of Books and Magazines and Other Materials About Both Computer Hardware and Software Being Manufactured All Over the World at Such a Rapid Rate (I.A.C.R.P.B.M.O.M.A.B.C.H.S.B.M.A.O.W.S.R.R.), in their eternal search for brevity, have created a set of Universal Symbols for Computer Reviewers and Publishers of Books and Magazines and Other Materials About Both Computer Hardware and Software Being Manufactured All Over the World at Such a Rapid Rate (U.S.C.R.P.B.M. O.M.A.B.C.H.S.B.M.A.O.W.S.R.R.).

Computers speak a universal language, and it is only fair that those who must write about computers should have a library of Universal Symbols at their disposal.

Peter A McWilliams
De Facto President

I.A.C.R.P.B.M.O.M.A.B.C.H.S.B.M.A.O.W.S.R.R.

Double-sided disk drive

 Computer will perform marriage ceremonies

 Computer plays synthesized dance music

 Suitable for a family

 Suitable for a rather strange family

 Suitable for a large family

 Suitable for a hungry family

Large file capacity

 Word processing capabilities

 Sold door to door by former encyclopedia salespersons

 Sophisticated

 Suitable for a couple

 Suitable for a rather strange couple

 Suitable for a couple who mess around

Suitable for a divorced couple

 Suitable for a male chauvinist

 Large memory

 Small memory

 Conforms to industry standards

 Does not conform to industry standards

 Apple

Palm (Made in California)

 Pair (Two disk drives)

 Peanut (Word processing program approved by Jimmy Carter)

 Lemon

 Turkey

 Fishy

 Multiplies fast

Stinks

 May drive you to drink

 For the birds

 Portable

 Semi-portable

 Normal size video screen

 Small video screen

Large video screen

 Very large video screen

 Costs a lot of dough, boy

 If you need to ask, you can't afford it

 Build it yourself

 Not designed for human beings

 Electronic mail

Do whatever is necessary to get this computer

 Confusing

 Gives off a lot of heat

 Save your money

 Hot

 Not so hot

 Not hot at all

Video games available

 Realistic video games

 Trashy

 May put you to sleep

 May make you sick

 Has no idea what times the planes arrive

 Six out of seven people want this computer but can't afford it.

My criteria for choosing computers, programs, and peripherals to review are simple.

First, I try to evaluate machines that are widely advertised and widely available. Some make poor word processors (Apple and Atari) and some make great word processors (IBM and DEC). I feel it's as important to steer people *away* from heavily-advertised poor values as it is to steer them *toward* not-so-heavily-advertised better values.

Which brings us to the second criterion: value. If a small company is turning out a product of exceptional value, I tend to gravitate towards that. I don't think anyone reading **The Word Processing Book** could have missed my admiration for The Word Plus. It is still not only the best spell-check program but, at $150, the best *value* in spell-check programs available today.

A third criterion is simply what people ask about. Although I keep no scientific records, I'm sure that a subconscious counter is clicking away the number of times people write asking about this computer or that program.

The fourth criterion is uniqueness. *The* most portable computer, or the *only* word processing program designed especially for screenwriters is likely to attract my attention.

The fifth criterion is price. I have arbitrarily decided to review computers costing $5,000 or less (not including printer or software). There is plenty of word processing power in the under-$5,000 category, and to go over that takes one into the world of *mini*-computers, which is another world entirely. Hence, I will not be reviewing the Fortune 32:16 or the new Corvus.

The sixth criterion is versatility. The machines should be able to do something other than word processing. I therefore stay away from "dedicated" or "stand alone" word processors. These machines (Lanier, Wang, IBM Display Writer) are utterly dependent upon the host company for revision, improvement, and expansion. Besides, they usually cost over $5,000.

The seventh criterion is screen and keyboard. An eighty-character screen and a detachable keyboard are so valuable for word processing — and there are so many wonderful, inexpensive personal computers that feature both — I tend to avoid personal computers that do not have them.

The final criterion is simply my own personal interests. I'm a lousy speller and spend no time footnoting, so I tend to pay more attention to spell-check programs than I do to footnote programs. I cannot pretend that *all* my criteria are objective. Frankly, I'm not sure if any of them are.

My hope is that, between **The Word Processing Book**, **The Personal Computer Book**, and comments in the buying guide, I will help to create educated consumers: people who will be able to look at computers and decide for themselves whether those machines would make good word processors or not. (Well, I can *hope*, can't I?)

* * * *

Let's look first at software, then at printers and finally at personal computers themselves.

SOFTWARE

The two most popular word processing programs for personal computers are WordStar and PeachText (formerly Magic Wand). In terms of sales and popularity, WordStar has the edge. Both are fine programs and each has its strengths and weaknesses. In general, WordStar's strengths lie in the area of editing and PeachText's strengths lie in the area of printing.

WordStar

If one had to choose an industry standard for word processing software it would be WordStar. All the features listed in *Chapter Three*, **The Wonders of Word Processing** are included with WordStar except a dictionary program, proportional spacing and kerning.

WordStar is a screen oriented program. What you see on the video screen is exactly the way the text will appear when printed, word for word, line for line, page for page.

Giving commands to WordStar one uses a standard key on all personal computers, the **control key**. With the control key depressed all the characters on the keyboard take on a new meaning. It's rather like sending your keyboard to est. The control key is depressed and, while depressed, one or two other keys are hit. In this way WordStar uses a standard keyboard to communicate 97 different commands.

If you were to type "KY," one would think you were discussing a lubricating jelly. If you type "KY" while depressing the control key, you would be telling WordStar that you wanted a certain block of text deleted. (The computer abbreviation for the control key is "^"."^KY" or "Control-KY" both mean "Depress the control key and hit "KY.")

To move the cursor, for example, you would press ^ E, ^ S, ^ D, or ^ X. The letters E, S, D and X form a diamond on the keyboard: E is on top, S is left, D is right and X is down. Hence, with WordStar, if you want to move the cursor up the screen you would press ^ E. If you wanted to move it left you would press ^ S. If you wanted to move it right you would press ^ D, and ^ X would move it down. Typists can do this with one hand, usually. The control key is located close to the E-S-D-X diamond on the keyboard. Hunt-and-peckers such as myself will find that two hands are necessary. (Some computers, such as Xerox, Otrona, and Osborne, have adapted WordStar so that cursor movement keys move the cursor.)

^ KB marks the beginning of a block of type; ^ KK marks the end. ^ KV moves the marked block to another part of the text. ^ OR sets the right margin, ^ OL sets the left. ^ G deletes a character, ^ T deletes a word, ^ Y deletes a whole line, and so on.

All this might seem confusing at first and rather hard to learn. Why not have some extra keys on the keyboard with those functions clearly labeled? Surely pressing a "Delete Character" key is easier than remembering "^ G." So it seems, but keep in mind that you would need a keyboard with at least 97 extra keys, all with little printing on them, saying things like "Save, exit to operating system," or "Read file into text." This would not only add to the cost, as it does with stand alone word processors, but it would also add to the confusion.

Further, once you know that ^ G means "delete

character" it's much faster to find ˆ G than a new key labeled "delete character." This is because a typist — even a poor one like me — already knows where "G" is. One need only learn the placement of one new key, the control key. It is easier for the mind to learn that "ˆ G equals delete character" than it is for the hand to learn the placement of a delete character key.

This is one reason programs that are advertised as "easy to learn" should be examined carefully. Programs that are easy to learn are often difficult to use. Imagine riding a bicycle on which the training wheels were never removed.

WordStar has a companion program, MailMerge, that is highly recommended if you want to print form letters or multiple copies of the same document.

WordStar is the product that put its manufacturer, MicroPro International, on the map. It is well supported, although in recent months they seem to be spending their corporate time developing programs that imitate existing programs from other manufacturers rather than keeping WordStar the best. They released, for example, a truly mediocre spelling program, SpellStar, rather than adding proportional spacing, footnoting, and other potential improvements to WordStar. It is doubtful, however, that they will ever let WordStar slip too far behind the competition.

PeachText

Magic Wand, a good and popular program, was purchased about a year ago by Peachtree Software, manufacturer of a line of business software that is highly respected in the industry. (IBM chose the Peachtree line of business software for their Personal Computer.)

Peachtree spent the first year removing bugs from Magic Wand and improving one of Magic Wand's primary claims to fame: proportional spacing. Then they changed the name to PeachText.

PeachText currently features all the capabilities listed in Chapter Three except a dictionary, page break display, double strike and strikeout (no loss there).

PeachText is a character-oriented word processing program. This means that what you see on the screen has no relation to what will be printed on paper, except that one word will follow another and sentences and paragraphs will begin as indicated. There is no way of knowing where pages will break, for example, without a test print-out.

When you buy PeachText it is customized for your keyboard. In this way cursor movement keys (these are keys with little arrows pointing up, down, left and right) can be used. PeachText makes maximum use of special function keys as well.

The manual is presented in a lesson-by-lesson logical format. This, too, has been one of the traditional strengths of Magic Wand.

The print functions on PeachText are very powerful. In addition to the aforementioned proportional spacing, Peach-Text supports nine — count 'em, nine — intensities of bold face printing.

> **This is level one.**
> **This is level two.**
> **This is level three.**
> **This is level four.**
> **This is level five.**
> **This is level six.**
> **This is level seven.**
> **This is level eight.**
> **This is level nine.**

PeachText also does kerning, which will move a single character a fraction of a millimeter to the right or to the left within a word on the printed page.

Unfortunately, PeachText does not have one of the simplest print commands, print pause. This would allow one to change print wheels to, say, italicize certain words. Double strike would also be useful for some typesetting situations.

PeachText allows for a choice when printing with justified right hand margins: microspacing (spacing between letters) or regular spacing (spaces placed between words only). Although microspacing looks better, tests indicate that regular spacing is easier to read.

Another interesting feature is Flush Right-
Ragged Left. Since Flush Left-Ragged Right is the
accepted standard for correspondence, sending out your letters
with ragged left margins give your missives that style, that
flair, that air of well-modulated independence that will make
them truly noticed or truly ignored. If you haven't already
guessed, this paragraph is using Flush Right-Ragged Left
margins.

As you can see, neither is the perfect program. One wishes in that moment between sleeping and waking, when the impossible becomes possible and all dreams come true, that MicroPro and Peachtree would join forces as Microtree or PeachPro and, taking the best from their respective programs, create WordText or PeachStar — Super Software that would help writers, secretaries and students everywhere in our never ending battle for truth, justice and the American way.

Easy Writer II

When IBM was selecting software to offer with their personal computer, they chose a program from Information Unlimited Software called Easy Writer that had been quite popular on the Apple. One does not know quite why IBM made this choice, but it was clearly the weakest link in their personal computer offering. (That and the placement of the shift key, which we'll discuss later.)

Critics of Easy Writer who were kind dubbed it Not-So-Easy Writer. Critics who were less kind called it Sleazy Writer. The word went out: If you buy the IBM Personal Computer, don't buy Easy Writer with it.

Into this maelstrom of bad publicity comes Information Unlimited Software (IUS) with a new word processing program, Easy Writer II. Easy Writer II is an excellent program, light years removed from Easy Writer 1. If you hear discussions about Easy Writer, make sure you ask if they mean Easy Writer 1 (now owned by IBM) or Easy Writer II. In this chapter I will be discussing Easy Writer II.

Easy Writer II is designed especially for the IBM Personal Computer. It will only run on the IBM, therefore if you want this program, you must also get an IBM.

Easy Writer II has a few features not available on either PeachText or WordStar (thus far. Keep in mind that serious word processing on personal computers has only been around for three-or-so years and that updates on software — like new editions of a book — are continually being released. These updates are available for a small portion of the purchase price, usually $15 to $35.)

One such EasyWriter II feature, invaluable to screenwriters, is the ability to switch from one preset margin to another to another. Easy Writer II does this with three keystrokes and a return. The program will memorize up to eight preset margins.

(Aside to screenwriters: Keep in mind that almost any program will print proper script formats. With WordStar, for example, you can center a character's name with three keystrokes, then type out action and dialog using the margins for action. The margins can then be reset—seven keystrokes to reset both left and right margins—and the dialog can be reformed, speech by speech. You can also invest $60 in Smartkey, discussed later, and have margin changes—even the character's name added—with the push of a single button.)

In addition to margins, EasyWriter II will also memorize other formatting commands such as decimal tabs, character pitch, and line spacing.

EasyWriter II is a screen oriented program — what you see on the screen is what you'll see on the paper. This is more true of EasyWriter II than with any other program I know. Since it's written especially for the IBM, words that are underlined display on the video screen as underlined, words that are in bold display in bold. (With other word processing programs, one puts what are known as **embedded commands** into the text. These display on the screen before and after the highlighted area. For example, if you wanted to print the word "word" in boldface, the screen on WordStar would display ˆ Bwordˆ B. In PeachText it would display @word@.

These embedded text commands can be switched off so that they will not display in WordStar. They cannot be switched off in PeachText.)

A drawback of EasyWriter II is that it does not store text in standard CP/M files, therefore the text can only be worked on by programs furnished by Information Unlimited Software. You could not, for example, use The WORD Plus to check the spelling of a document. (IUS offers a very good spell-check program called EasySpeller, although it's not as good as The WORD Plus.) It is not even certain that you can use text manipulation programs written especially for the IBM. (Some work, and some do not.)

The reasons for all this are given later in the chapter when I discuss the IBM Personal Computer. Keep in mind that what you gain in features you may lose in flexibility.

In all, though, EasyWriter II is a fine word processing program, well worthy of your consideration.

The EasyWriter II people have added a unique level of support to their software. For 20% of the purchase price (about $70 for EasyWriter II) you get unlimited use of a toll-free help line for one full year. This is invaluable when learning a program. Let's hope more software houses follow Information Unlimited's lead. IUS has also introduced EasyFiler, a sophisticated filing system that interfaces with EasyWriter II.

Volkswriter

This is a new, inexpensive ($195) word processing program written especially for the IBM Personal Computer. While I have not had a chance to evaluate it, it is getting a good reputation among IBMophiles.

Select

Select is a program that is easy to learn, but cumbersome to use. Further, it doesn't begin to approach the power of, say, WordStar.

The strength of Select is an excellent interactive tutorial that comes with each program. This tutorial takes a person in gradual and enjoyable steps through the various features of the program. The "student" is encouraged to "give it a try" each step of the way. If one accomplishes the task correctly the student is rewarded with, "WOW! Am I impressed!" or "You're HOT!" If one fails, however, he or she is chided with, "Have you ever felt like the ship was sailing without you? Please go back and give it one more try." or "If you can't get this one you're looking out the window."

Using this tutorial, within an hour or so one could be successfully processing words using Select.

The problem comes after you've used Select continuously for several weeks. Select is what I call a **multi-screen program**. This means that you enter text on one screen, then must switch screens to do any editing of the entered text. If you've typed a sentence, look at it on the screen, and see that a letter needs replacing, rather than simply going back to that letter and changing it, you must exit the "text entry" screen and enter the "edit" screen. After the correction has been made, you must exit the edit screen and once again return to the text entry screen.

Select is rather like a tool kit with lots and lots of easy to learn tools and a jolly Mr. Goodwrench to teach you how to use them. If you use tools infrequently, this will serve you well. If you use tools often, the bending and reaching and constant manipulation of tools can become annoying.

Select is a great word processing program for those who do little word processing. It's easy to learn and easy to relearn. And if you only use a hammer to pound a few tacks every week, you'll never find yourself longing for a hydraulic staple gun.

Scriptsit II

Whereas WordStar is difficult to learn but easy to use and Select is easy to learn but difficult to use, Scriptsit II is difficult to learn and difficult to use.

Scriptsit II is a multi-screen program and can be run only on Radio Shack computers. The files are not CP/M but TRSDOS (Tandy Radio Shack Disk Operating

System). This means that the text can only be manipulated with programs written for Radio Shack computers. It is even more cumbersome to operate than Select and at least as difficult to learn as WordStar.

Despite its many drawbacks it does offer a few features that most word processing programs do not, among them proportional spacing, margin memory (see EasyWriter II above), and a phrase storer. (The latter stores phrases that can later be added to the text.)

If you already have a Radio Shack computer, Scriptsit II might be a good choice. If you do not, it does not come highly recommended. (See comments about Radio Shack computers later in this chapter.)

Perfect Writer

Let us begin by accepting the fact that there *is* no perfect word processing program. Word processing is still dominated by tradeoffs ("In order to have this you can't have that") and personal tastes (some people like pushing special buttons to implement commands, others like a control key followed by a familiar character on the keyboard).

Perfection, in fact, is probably impossible. Like audio, state-of-the-art is the most one can hope for.

Is Perfect Writer, then, at least a state-of-the-art Writer? Well, it's headed in the right direction. Let's hope the creator(s) of this program do not take the program's name too much to heart: it is, by definition, impossible to improve upon perfection.

Perfect Writer has some useful features not offered by, say, WordStar. You can split the screen and edit two files simultaneously, moving text from one file to another if you like. It does true proportional spacing. It creates indexes and handles complicated footnoting.

It is not, however, a true screen-oriented program. Because it offers so many print and formatting options, what you see on the screen is not necessarily what you'll get on the printed page.

The documentation is excellent, the finest I have

read. Clear, well-illustrated, understandable, with occasional flashes of — would you believe it? — humor.

It is a first-rate program, one worthy of your careful consideration.

Spellbinder

Contrary to its name, Spellbinder is not a spell-check program. It is, in fact, a word processing program, and a good one too.

Like PeachText, the strength of Spellbinder lies in its printing. True proportional spacing, even typesetting printers (like the Sanders) are fully supported. (Oddly enough, as powerful as its printing capabilities are, it will not underline *and* boldface, or doublestrike *and* underline at the same time.)

Whenever a word processing program is powerful in printing, it usually sacrifices something in editing. The most obvious sacrifice is the lack of screen orientation. What you see on the screen while you're editing is not what you're likely to get on the paper. A preview mode, however, allows you to see how the text will look before it is printed, but to make any changes you must exit the preview mode and re-enter the edit mode. The what-you-see-is-what-you-get-while-editing feature is more important to some than to others.

Another editing weakness is the inability to insert while inserting. If you were, for example, inserting the line "We all had a nice day," and decided to back up and add "very" before "nice," you could not do it. You would have to leave the insert mode, return to the edit mode, move the cursor to the space before "nice," go back to the insert mode, and add "very."

In a sense, Spellbinder is a two-screen program, although not as cumbersome to use as, say, Select.

While we're on the subject of possible (I say possible because you might not mind any of these) drawbacks, managing very large files (files larger than the RAM of the computer) is less transparent than it is in, say, WordStar. For most letters, chapters, and articles, this will not pose a problem. For managing large mailing lists, it might be difficult. (I have mailing lists on a hard disk computer that are more than 400K. The computer itself has 64K on RAM, and editing large mailing lists like that would not be a simple task with Spellbinder. You cannot, for example, scroll backwards through a long file.)

Now the good stuff, and the reasons why some people think that Spellbinder is the best word processor around. To begin with, Spellbinder will (with the above exceptions) do everything listed in the chapter on **The Wonders of Word Processing**. Spellbinder is installed to use the function keys of most keyboards. Cursor movement keys move the cursor, and the computer takes on a more stand-alone word processor feel.

Spellbinder also has something known as *macros*. Macros are mini-programs that can be invoked with a keystroke or two. They allow the program to perform complicated, individualized functions with a minimum of effort. Because it's a program within a program, a macro provides specific customization and allows a wide variety of uses. (All those "special case" things you need to have done that no other word processor offers, you might be able to do with Spellbinder — but make sure it can before you buy.)

Although macros are a marvelous concept, I wish Spellbinder had a more structured way of "selling" them. Some dealers know how to write them, many don't. Simple macros can be gotten by calling Spellbinder's customer support department. There is no system for having complex micros written. Several popular macros are included with the program (some of them discussed below). A disk of the most frequently requested macros, and a system (so much per hour of programming time, for example) for customized macro writing would be a real plus.

Among the useful print options is the ability to print directly from the screen. With most word processing programs, the text must be saved on a disk and the file then printed from the disk. This is not much of an effort, but for labels, memos, and notes, direct printing from the screen is a convenience.

The supplied macros with Spellbinder include form generation and mail list management functions (alphabetizing, sorting by zip code, and so on) that many will find useful.

Also supplied are a variety of math functions (figures can be added across rows or down columns), and fixed point arithmetic.

In all, it's a powerful program worthy of your consideration.

Scriptor

Another program I have not seen is Scriptor. It is written with the screenwriter in mind. It formats text created with any CP/M-based word processing program to any of the various script formats. Were I a screen writer, I would certainly investigate this program.

Grammatik

This is a remarkable program that flags possible grammar and punctuation errors and even makes suggestions for correcting them. The effectiveness of Grammatik (pronounced gra-MAH-tic, as in "grammatical" without the "al") surprised me.

The text of this book has gone through two professional copy editors, two nonprofessional (though nonetheless paid) ones, two nonprofessional nonpaid ones, my mother and myself. In addition, letters from kindly strangers pointing out errors in the first edition of this book were duly massaged into the text. And along came Grammatik.

I thought it might be cute if a computer program found a mistake or two in the book. Cute? This thing is vicious. Not since Freshman Comp has my writing been so marked-up and questioned. Actually I didn't mind — much. I was, in fact, amazed and delighted and only occasionally defensive.

It began in the third paragraph of Chapter One. It suggested putting a question mark inside a set of quotation marks. It was right.

Then it picked apart the beginning of the fourth

paragraph, "In the last five years all of this has changed." It claimed that "all of this" is a wordy phrase and suggested that I simply use "all this." Again, it was right. "In the last five years all this has changed." is a better sentence.

Then it pointed out a misuse of "a while." (Should have been "awhile.") It said, "referred to as" is a wordy phrase and suggested "called." It recommended that I drop "of the envelope" in the sentence, "I must have received dozens of these, proclaiming on the outside of the envelope..." Again, it was right.

It pointed out that I am addicted to the word "very." Each time the word came up it was flagged for being a "vague adverb." I must have removed 30 "verys" from this book. It also flagged "upon," telling me it was "archaic." Well, my dictionary says it is "infrequently used" not "archaic," and I like it better than "on," so dozens of "upons" remain.

It tagged Xerox and Coke, told me they were trademarks, and suggested "photocopy" and "cola." (I like Xerox and Coke.) It said the phrase "reason why" was redundant which, of course, it is. It found a double "the" in a sentence ("it tells you that the the word...") that escaped everyone else. And on and on and on. Grammatik is responsible for more than fifty improvements in this book.

It was fun, though, to catch the taskmaster at its own task. It flagged the word "sort of" and labeled it a "wordy phrase." It suggested using either "somewhat" or "rather." If, however, one were to use "rather," it would later be tagged by Grammatik as a "vague adverb."

Grammatik is available with or without a spell-check program. Although its spell-check program is good, The WORD Plus is better.

Grammatik is available for Radio Shack, IBM and all CP/M computers. It costs $75.

Punctuation and Style

An even better program for checking punctuation and grammar is the latest brainchild from the creator of The Word Plus, Wayne Holder.

The program is divided into two parts. The first

part is called CLEANUP. This checks for punctuation errors, double words, capitalization errors, and makes sure that quotation marks, brackets, and other things that *should* come in pairs *do* come in pairs.

The second part is called PHRASE. PHRASE will find over 500 overused or frequently misused phrases, point them out, and suggest alternate (or correct) substitutions.

The idea behind dividing the program into two parts is that, once learned, the PHRASE part of the program will seldom need to be used. However, the errors in CLEANUP are often typos, and even the best grammarian may want to run his or her every letter through CLEANUP.

Both CLEANUP and PHRASE, unlike Grammatik, will mark the errors you want to change in the text. (With Grammatik you need a printed copy to mark changes on, then go back and find the changes in the text.)

On the whole, Punctuation and Style seems a more complete, sophisticated program than Grammatik, and at $125, it is highly recommended.

Keep in mind, however, that no program can check the grammar in a sentence that requires logical (ie: human) analysis. Nothing will replace a reading or two of *On Writing Well*. Even elaborate programs on mainframe computers designed to "improve" the written word can't be fully trusted.

One of these programs at the Bell Laboratories changed "Fourscore and seven years ago, our forefathers brought forth upon this continent a new nation, conceived in liberty and dedicated to the proposition that all men are created equal..." into "Eighty-seven years ago, our grandfathers created a free nation here."

Some things are best left to the word processor in the human mind.

The Random House Thesaurus

But don't lose any sleep over Grammatik's lost glory. The Grammatik people have now joined Dictronics, and Dictronics has come out with an excellent program that has, thus far, no competition. This is a beautiful (handsome, comely, seemly, attractive, lovely, pretty, fine) program. It is well thought out, intelligent (bright, clever, alert, discerning, shrewd, smart), yet simply presented.

I have not used a thesaurus five times in the past fifteen years, and yet I still find myself excited (ruffled, discomposed, perturbed, stimulated, agitated, eager, enthusiastic) about this program.

To use the Random House Thesaurus (Random House has no connection with the program, other than the money they make from their license to Dictronics) one places the cursor within the word that needs, uh, thesaurusizing, pushes the ESCAPE key twice, and within a second or two the top of the screen is filled with synonyms.

Select the synonym you want, move the cursor to that word, push the ESCAPE key again, and the program automatically replaces the original word with the newly selected word. If the original word was the best, the RETURN key returns you to the word processing program with nothing changed.

That it works as well and as effortlessly as it does covers the positive aspects of the word "excited" (stimulated, eager, enthusiastic.) The negative aspects of my excitement (ruffled, discomposed, perturbed, agitated) stem from the limitations of the program.

As I see them, the limitations are two. The first is that The Random House Thesaurus currently works only with WordStar and PeachText — fine for WordStar and PeachText users, but what about the rest of the universe? (Soon to be released is a version that will work with any word processing program running on the IBM Personal Computer.)

The second limitation is that the full thesaurus takes 240K of disk capacity. Hence, to place a dictionary program *and* a thesaurus *and* a word processing program on one disk (assuming the second disk drive would be used for document files), would require a disk with more than 500K. And I remember when I thought 340K per drive was ostentatious.

The Dictronics folk are working on adapting The

Random House Thesaurus to other word processing programs, and if I were them, I would have chosen WordStar and PeachText, too. They are, after all, the most popular and widely used word processing programs in the world.

There doesn't seem to be much way of getting around the disk capacity question. They fit a 60,000 word thesaurus into 240K, and that's pretty good. (They make special smaller versions — with less words, of course — in forms as small as 80K.) Those of us who want it all may have to bite the bullet and get large capacity drives, or even a hard disk.

In the mean time, I leave the thesaurus on the same disk as the word processing program, put my document files on another disk drive, and switch disks when it's time to spell-check. (The thesaurus is used throughout the editing process, the spell-check program less frequently.)

The Random House Thesaurus is $150.

Micro Link II

This is an easy to use, inexpensive communication package for almost any computer. It allows one computer to transfer information to and from another computer, or allows one computer to hook up to data bank services through a modem.

There are a great many communications programs around. I include this one because of its simplicity and price ($89).

SuperFile

SuperFile is a remarkable program that lets you file any information — from a word to a book — under as many as 250 different key words.

You can file a letter under not just who it was to or what it was about or the date written or who wrote the letter, but under all four — plus 246 other classifications. *Simultaneously.*

An address can be filed under not just last name, but first name, occupation, city, state, zip code, area code,

likes, dislikes, where you met them, whether you ever want to meet them again, and 239 other vital statistics.

Quotes can be filed under who said them, when they were said, and 248 different subject categories.

Books, articles, photographs, music — anything you would not want to, or would not be able to, put into the computer — can be numbered, and that number filed under as many as 250 key words. For example, "Photo #1256" could be filed under the key words "waterfall, Canada, color, nature, 35mm," and hundreds more. Anytime you asked for photos of a waterfall, or scenes of Canada, or shots of nature, "Photo #1256" would be listed.

And now comes the best part. Not only does it file a bit of information in 250 categories simultaneously, it also allows you to combine key word requests. Only those bits of information that match *all* requested categories will appear.

If you were a classical music buff, Superfile could tell you how many hundred recordings of Beethoven's Fifth Symphony you had by simply asking for "BEETHOVEN *and* FIFTH SYMPHONY." The several you might have by Toscanini could be found by typing in "BEETHOVEN *and* FIFTH SYMPHONY *and* TOSCANINI."

You could ask SuperFile to search through your electronic address book and find all of your FRIENDS living in CLEVELAND who own a COMPUTER. Only those entries with the key words "friends," "computer," and "Cleveland" would be presented.

Further, a file can be created from a sorted list that allows you, using certain word processing programs, to add the information, automatically, into form letters. (WordStar is one of them. You can contact the SuperFile people for details on others.)

SuperFile is easy to use and, compared with other data base management programs, inexpensive. ($195.) It carries an unprecedented 30-day money back guarantee. Use the program for 30 days. If you don't like it, send it back for a full refund. With the ease of copying a program disk and Xeroxing an instruction manual, it's nice to see a software company that actually *trusts* its customers.

Smartkey

Another program, that operates on any CP/M computer, is Smartkey. Smartkey allows you to make any key on your keyboard any other key. Great for the Dvorak keyboard, or inventing your own keyboard arrangement. You can also program any key to become a whole series of instructions. The " ` " key, for example, can become a series of commands that resets both left and right margins. The " ~ " key can return them to their original locations. This allows screenwriters, secretaries, accountants, etc. to reset margins with one keystroke.

Each key can be made to represent up to 200 characters, so short, frequently-used phrases can be assigned a key (book titles, names, addresses, etc.). This means that hitting one key can enter your name, address and phone number—complete with carriage returns—providing it's under 200 characters. Smartkey is $60.

TeleVideo Software

Those who have purchased—or are considering the purchase—of a TeleVideo 802 may want to get a program from New Generation Systems. It allows for easy programming of the programmable function keys, which eases the operation of many programs. It also works with all TeleVideo 950 terminals, and retails for $75.

There are two other programs that adapt function keys on the TeleVideo 802 computer and 950 terminal to WordStar. One is NuKey from Business Solutions, Inc. The other is TVI 2000 Conversion from Word Tech Systems.

Of the three, TVI 2000 is the best. It has a microchip that installs in the keyboard (don't worry: if I can do it, you can do it). The other programs are software driven, and therefore cannot overcome the problem built into the TeleVideo keyboard: The cursor movement keys are the same as some WordStar commands.

TVI 2000 solves this. You cannot, however, select which function keys control which functions, something you *can* do with the other two programs. If you want cursor movement keys and predetermined function keys (there are dozens of functions programmed in), then get TVI 2000. If you want to program your own function keys, and don't care about cursor movement keys (or are willing to relearn some WordStar commands), then investigate NuKey and the one from New Generation Systems.

PRINTERS
Epson

The Epson MX-80 is generally considered to be the best dot matrix printer in its price range ($500-$1,000). Of all the inexpensive dot matrix printers available, IBM chose the Epson as the printer for the IBM Personal Computer. The label says IBM, but the printer is Epson MX-80.

A dot matrix printer, for reasons detailed in the last chapter, should be considered for word processing only if the final appearance of printed copy need not look impressive.

Another reason for a dot matrix printer, particularly the MX-80, is that it travels well. Compact and weighing only twelve pounds, the MX-80 could be slipped into almost any suitcase. The MX-80 combined with one of the more portable computers listed below makes a great on-the-road word processor with full printing capabilities.

The MX-80 uses pins to feed continuous form paper. If you want to use letterhead stationery or single sheets of paper you'll need to buy the MX-80 FT.

SMITH-CORONA TP-1

The Smith-Corona TP-1 is made by one of the largest manufacturers of portable typewriters in the world. The TP-1 is Smith-Corona's first venture into the world of personal computer printers. Not surprisingly, the TP-1 resembles, in look and quality of construction, a portable electric typewriter with the keyboard removed.

The Smith-Corona TP-1 prints at the unspectacular speed of 12 characters per second. It does, however, use a daisy wheel (eleven type styles currently available) and prints sharp, uniform letter quality letters.

A letter on a 55 cps NEC Spinwriter might take a minute to print. That same letter on the TP-1 would take almost five. It is also not in the same league as the NEC in terms of rugged construction.

The TP-1 is, however, relatively inexpensive. It retails for $895, and is frequently discounted to somewhere between $500 and $600. In other words, it is a letter quality printer at a dot matrix price.

For the writer on a limited budget who needs to print only letters and occasional manuscripts, the TP-1 would be a good choice. For a business, or for a large-volume writer, the TP-1 might prove too slow. (The hourly cost of someone standing over a printer chugging away must be considered.)

Weighing only 18.5 pounds, the TP-1 would make an excellent traveling companion. (NEC Spinwriters weigh 45.5 pounds.)

If money is limited, and quality output is important, the TP-1 is a good choice.

Brother HR-1 (also Comrex CR-1)

The Brother HR-1 (also sold as the Comrex CR-1) is a bit faster than the Smith-Corona TP-1 (17 vs 12 characters per second), a bit quieter in operation, and, naturally, costs a bit more. ($1,150, although, like the Smith-Corona, it tends to be discounted.)

As of this writing, this is the least expensive letter-quality printer that will work with WordStar. (WordStar does not have a printer driver for the Smith-Corona, and Smith-Corona has not emulated any of the printers Word-Star supports.)

The Brother and the Comrex will do double strike, bold, and underline. They will not do proportional printing, super scripting or sub scripting.

Bytewriter

The Bytewriter is an Olivetti Praxis 30 electric typewriter with an interface that makes it a computer printer. It prints at about 10 characters per second. The cost is $695.

When not printing, the Bytewriter functions like the Olivetti Praxis typewriter it is.

If you need a typewriter *and* a printer *and* you're on a budget, this would be the printer to get.

Diablo and Qume

While Diablo and Qume both make fine printers, if you're going to spend that much money, my suggestion is to buy an NEC. This is based upon the superior reliability NECs over the years. The NEC is a workhorse.

If, however, you need a special feature offered by Diablo or Qume, or if you can get it for a special price, you will not be displeased with either printer.

Daisywriter

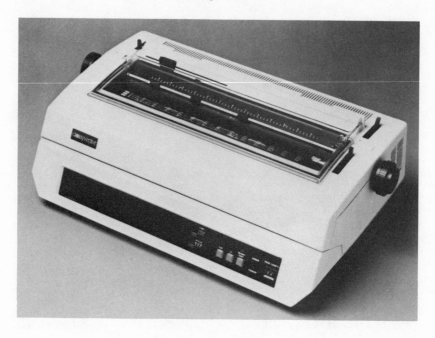

The Daisywriter is the least-expensive full-featured letter quality printer available. It will do true proportional printing, microspacing, superscripts, and subscripts. The Daisywriter retails for $1,495.

The Daisywriter features a 48K buffer, which allows you to enter the file to be printed into the *printer's* memory. While the printer is printing from its memory, your computer is free to be used for other tasks.

NEC

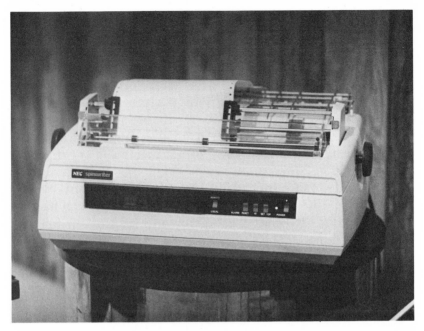

The NEC Spinwriter is a letter quality printer with an excellent reputation for print quality and durability. Time and time again I have heard unsolicited praise for the Spinwriter from people who know printers and have no vested interest in NEC or any other computer printer.

The Spinwriters print at a top speed of 55 characters per second, the fastest rated speed of any letter quality printer in its price range (around $2,500). A 35 CPS model is available that has all the Spinwriter features except speed, and this retails for about $1,700.

Printers and software are the most frequently discounted part of any personal computer system. Even if a dealer does not give discounts on the computer he or she will frequently take something off the printer.

All the above NEC prices include a device known as a tractor. A tractor pulls the paper through the printer by little pins on the left and right side of the page. This special perforated paper is known as **tractor paper** or **continuous form feed paper**. It's relatively endless so that page after page can be printed without stopping. It's good for rough drafts and for printing invoices, checks, and so forth.

Tractor paper is usually not of the best quality, but high-quality stationery can be glued or tipped onto standard tractor paper. This allows letter after letter to be printed without stopping to change paper after each sheet. This tipping process costs about $50 per thousand sheets and will work with envelopes, too. It's a good compromise between hand feeding and the expense of an automatic sheet feeder (about $1,500-$3,500).

If you don't mind feeding the sheets you print one at a time, rather like loading a standard typewriter, you can get the Spinwriter without the tractor and save about $200. If you're planning to use the printer for business applications right away, a tractor is recommended. If you might or might not use one eventually, the tractor can easily be added later.

Printer Recommendations

After working with a good number of letter quality printers, I can recommend that, if you plan to spend more than $1,000 on a letter quality printer, spend a few hundred more and get an NEC.

The Smith Corona TP-1 is noisy and slow, but at least it's cheap. For about $550 you can get letter quality printing. It's a boon to people on a budget. It's hard to recommend spending an extra $1,000 when $550 seems high. (A TP-2 has been announced. This will no doubt offer some improvements. I have not been given the details. Also, one can expect lower prices for the remaining TP-1s in the marketplace.)

The $1,000-$1,500 printers (Brother, Comrex, Daisy-writer, etc.) all seem to have the same print mechanism and, my heavens, is it slow (rated anywhere from 12 to 16 CPS). The overall quality and sturdiness seem to be less than the NECs. The tractor feeds have trouble handling tipped-on (glued on) stationery (NECs seem to have no trouble).

And all three machines have the most irritating platen

feeds (the round knobs on the side that you turn when putting paper into the printer). You can't just turn them, like you would on a typewriter. You must push in and *then* turn, all the while continuing to push. This is what one must do to the right one. The left one does not seem to work no matter what you do. I cannot see the sense, reason, or purpose for this. One thing that's not difficult to see: it's damn inconvenient.

The more expensive printers (Diablo, Qume, Starwriter F-10 and Printmaster F-10), have the speed of the NECs, have normal platen feeders, but do not seem to have the print quality or the ruggedness. And they usually cost the same—and maybe more—than the NECs.

The printed product of any of the above printers will look fine. No one will look at your correspondence and say, "You certainly should have bought a better printer!" I doubt if anyone will be able to tell the final printing from an expensive electric typewriter.

Sometimes there are system prices that include one of the above printers. Sometimes the dealer will trade the system printer for another of your choice, and sometimes not. Sometimes the system price is too good to pass up. Be sure to investigate printer speed, operation, and quality with the same attention you spend on your computer.

And now, for my answer to the most frequently-asked question about printers (if my mail is any indicator): Can I use my electric typewriter as a printer? The answer: Maybe.

If you have a Selectric, or other ball-type ("typing element") electric typewriter, I would advise against it. These machines, when subjected to the full-out demands of computer printing, tend to be unreliable. My suggestion: Sell the Selectric before prices drop on used Selectrics, and buy a computer printer, *or* keep the Selectric for notes or labels or old times sake, and buy a computer printer.

If you have an old-style electric that has a separate piece of metal for each letter (like a manual typewriter with a motor added), the cost of converting that to a computer printer can be a lot. When you're done, you'll have more reliability than the Selectric-type (probably), but is the total cost really worth it? It might be better to spend a bit more and get an inexpensive printer.

Many of the newer electronic typewriters, the kind that use daisy wheels, make reliable printers. Many were designed, in fact, to hook up to a computer, and these generally work fine. If, however, connecting an electronic typewriter—daisy wheel or no—to a computer voids your typewriter warranty, I wouldn't suggest it. The typewriter company knows something about its machine as a computer printer that we don't, and that something might be that the typewriter when used as a printer is not too reliable.

A printer stand.

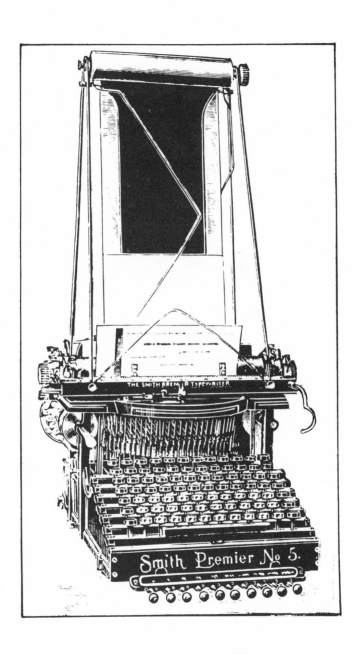

Timex/Sinclair

Clive Sinclair is one of those Britishers, like Freddie Laker, who wants to bring to the masses the playthings of the rich. For Freddie Laker it was transatlantic travel. For Clive Sinclair, it's personal computers.

For almost three years, Sinclair has been selling by mail a computer that was far less than anyone thought computers could possibly sell for. If it broke, you put it in an envelope, mailed it back, and they sent you a new one.

Timex, of course, is the company that, many years ago, decided watches should not be the exclusive domain of jewelers. They sold watches for far less that anyone thought possible. If it didn't work, you mailed it back and they sent you a new one.

Now they have joined forces, these two: the marketing might of Timex and the simple computer design of Sinclair — the Timex/Sinclair. They expect to sell millions of them. They probably will.

There are TV commercials planned. John Cameron Swayze is on a firing range. He straps a Timex/Sinclair to a target. The marksmen shoot, shattering the plastic case. A scientist in a white lab coat walks over to the

Timex/Sinclair and computes the value of pi to the 32nd decimal point. Swayze looks into the camera, holding up the battered remains of the Timex/Sinclair. "The Timex/Sinclair," he says. "Takes a shooting but keeps on computing."

Someone has called the Timex/Sinclair the world's first disposable computer. They may be right. I'm not sure how long anyone over the age of fifteen will use this computer before either (a) buying a better computer, or (b) giving up on personal computing altogether.

The computer has a smaller-than-full-size membrane keyboard. It plugs into any TV, although the display is limited to monochrome, even on a color set. The ability to do BASIC programming is built-in, as are 2K of RAM. Programs can be entered through the keyboard, or loaded through a standard cassette player (which you supply).

A printer ($100) saves what you've programmed, although the print-quality is, in a word, bad. An additional 16K of memory is $50. A modem, which allows one to contact The Source or CompuServe, is $100.

For a young person fascinated by programming (as opposed to the arcade games), this would be a frequently-used possession.

The VIC-20, at $200, features a full-sized keyboard, push-button (as opposed to membrane) keys, color display, arcade games, and much more. It's a better inexpensive computer, but for many, $200 may be too much.

I have mixed feelings about the Timex/Sinclair. On one hand, I'm glad that this much computing power is available for people — particularly young people — who can't afford more. On the other hand, I'm afraid that too many people will buy one, play with it for a week, and abandon the concept of personal computing altogether. These same people, had they invested in a better-quality machine, might have used computers daily.

As a way to contact The Source or CompuServe, it's quite inexpensive. However, if cost is a major consideration in computing, you might want to think twice about data banks. The minimum rate is around $5 per hour. (And that's after midnight. Most people, particularly young people, will want to use data banks during the evening hours, at almost $8 per hour.) Time flies on data banks and, like long distance phone calls to a lover, they can quickly add up. One could spend on data banks in a month the cost of a Timex/Sinclair with modem.

The programs offered for the Timex/Sinclair are varied and numerous, and likely to become more so. (For the most part, the programs come printed in a book. One copies the program into the machine and saves it on a cassette tape. When one wants to run that program again, he or she simply plays the tape. It's an awkward, but economical, procedure. Some people enjoy it.) There's even — Heaven help us — a word processing program.

The Timex/Sinclair will be well supported, simply because there will be so many of them around. It's fun. It's cheap. But comparing a Timex/Sinclair to some of the other more powerful personal computers is like comparing a Harley Davidson with a moped.

Main assembly room for Timex/Sinclairs

Apple, Atari, Radio Shack, and Commodore

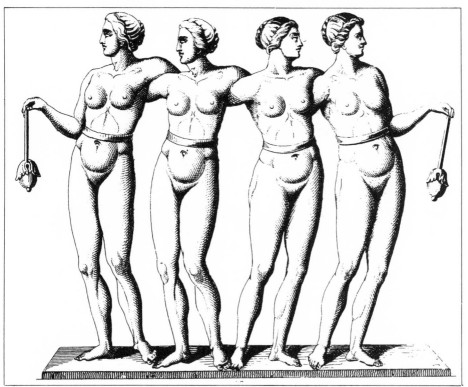

And a smooth-faced Atari executive, in charge of the Home Consumer Division, tears his gaze away from his in-office video screen and game master control to grin, "I play about 20 to 30 hours a day. If I had my druthers, I'd probably play all day long."—*San Francisco Examiner & Chronicle.*

The word Atari comes from the ancient Japanese game of GO. It's a board game, and when one player feels the surge of victory on his or her side, that player yells "ATARI!" The other player, struggling to avoid the "agony of defeat," might try any last minute maneuvers, but they usually fail. "ATARI!" is a cry of inevitable victory.

At the Atari Computer Company, each time favorable sales figures are released, all the employees go up on the rooftop and yell across the expanse of Silicon Valley, "ATARI!" At the other end of Silicon Valley, all the employ-

"Atari!"

ees of the Apple Computer Company respond by getting up on their roof and shouting, "SCREW YOU!" And the computer games continue.

I'm going to lump the four most popular computers together because I have basically the same thing to say about all four of them:

1. The computers are not so hot.
2. The support is terrific.

If you want to join a preformed, ongoing computer community, buy any of these machines. You'll find magazines, clubs, books, software, retail stores, and peripherals galore.

You may not wind up with the best computer, dollar-for-dollar, that you could have gotten, but you'll find a *family*. In some cases you'll find a cult, the members of which will be saying nasty things about me after reading this section.

I wish some great computers got the support that these machines have; or I wish these companies would come up with some great computers again.

I say "again" because, at one time, their computers were as good as any around, which is why they got so popular. Times have changed, and The Four Sisters have not changed with them.

The Apple II was introduced in 1977. That's not exactly what you would call "state-of-the-art," other than the art of preserving the past and selling it as the future.

The same is true of the personal computers marketed by the other three as well: What was a value in personal computers two or three or four years ago is ho-hum today.

And yet, it's because they've been around for several years, that there is so much support for them today. The more machines in the field, and the longer they're out there, the more programs and peripherals are offered — not only by the computer-maker, but by manufacturers of all kinds. Clubs form, magazines are published, books are written.

Like the chicken and the egg, the machines sell the software and the software sells the machines, and nobody is going to make obsolete the chicken that's been laying the golden eggs until the last moment.

And so, increasing amounts of money are spent on advertising, and a company leans a bit too heavily on its reputation.

For some, however, state-of-the-art technology is not as important as having someone to call when the program won't load — be it a friend who owns the same machine, or a fellow club member, or the salesperson who's been selling the same machine for so long that he or she knows it inside out.

For some, a monthly magazine (or two, or three) about nothing else but *their computer*, is more important than a sharper video display.

For some, a broad selection of programs more than makes up for a narrower selection of keys on the keyboard.

This selection of programs is especially important when it comes to full-color graphic games. These so-called

arcade games are available, for the most part, for the Atari and the Apple. Radio Shack with its Color Computer, and Commodore with its VIC-20, do have a selection of games — but if you want Pac-Man, it's Atari, and if you want Raster Blaster, well, you can run it on any computer you want, as long as it's an Apple.

(WARNING: Pac-Man on a coin-operated machine is not the same game as the home version of Pac-Man from Atari. Not only are the graphics sharper on the coin-operated version, but the game is more complex. Devoted video game players still play on coin-operated machines.)

I want you to be aware of the choice between support and state-of-the-art. There's only one computer company that seems to be building toward both, and that's IBM. (Discussed later in this chapter.) Unfortunately, IBM is on the expensive side, as home personal computers go.

If you choose one of The Big Four, you are choosing support. It's not a bad choice or a wrong choice. For many people entering the world of personal computers for the first time, it may be the best choice.

There is a great deal to learn when one gets his or her first computer. The more information available from a broad variety of sources, the easier learning that computer will be. That could be more important to you than 160 extra kilobytes of disk capacity for the same price, or a computer housing that isn't grey.

This is especially true if you live in a small town and your only contact with personal computers is a Radio Shack Computer Center, a computer store that only sells Apple and Commodore, and a department store that carries Atari.

Radio Shack Model 12

Radio Shack has come out with a Model 12. This is the only Radio Shack I would recommend for word processing. The whole unit seems a bit bland, a bit big, and a bit overpriced (Radio Shack is the Chevrolet of computers), but if Radio Shack is the only computer store in town, you could do worse for word processing or general office computing than the Model 12. (You could do worse without leaving Radio Shack.) The Model 12 does represent an overall improvement for Radio Shack, and they deserve a qualified pat on the back. (Pat, pat. Now let's move on.)

The Apple IIe and Lisa

The Apple computer has not been a good value for at least two years. Both the Apple II and Apple III have been overpriced, when compared with similarly featured computers on the market, since 1980.

That much has been common knowledge in the computer industry for some time, but the defenders of the Apple, those sentimentalists who bought an Apple II in 1977 or 1978 when it *was* a good value, always seem to end their anti-Apple comments with a slow nod and the comment, "But wait until the new Apples come out."

Well, I waited, and waited, and waited, and they are finally out. I could not be more underwhelmed. The Lisa? Yawn. The Apple IIe? Zzzzzz.

The Apple IIe (they say the e stands for enhanced. I

The Apple is highly recommended in some circles.

All right, I'll buy an Apple.

"Duh, an Apple, huh? Sounds good to me."

say it stands for expensive) added a few keys, lowercase letters, a bit more memory, and a printer port; reduced the number of chips (which has no value to the consumer, but makes it less expensive to produce), and raised the price (from $1,330 to $1,395). Even I, who have little faith in Apple, thought they were going to offer more and charge less.

Keep in mind that that price does not include a screen, or a disk drive, or one piece of software. By the time you add a monochrome screen, an 80-column display (it currently has 40), a numeric keypad, a fan, two modest disk drives, and enough software to do either word processing *or* electronic spreadsheeting, an Apple IIe would cost you more than $3,000. Compare the features available on other $3,000 computers. You'll see why I think the e stands for expensive, if not extortion.

The main reason people buy Apple IIs is because of software and peripherals produced by *other manufacturers*. Most of this comes from the salad days of the late 1970s when the Apple II was the only color computer on the block. This reason is driven home in millions of dollars of advertising every month ("Will Somebody Please Tell Me What an Apple Will Do?" etc.). (I've always wondered, "Will somebody please tell me why an Apple will do.")

The fact is, if you look at the telephone-directory sized listing of 16,000 programs available for the Apple, the vast majority of them are worthless. They look like entries in a high school program writing contest. ("You boys and girls will have 3 hours to write a computer program. Go.") The worthwhile Apple programs, from a business standpoint, have been rewritten for the IBM PC.

Alas, the one area in which Apple still has a stranglehold on programming is education. Apple sells computers to school systems very cheap. They know that for every Apple they place in the classroom, 40 active youngsters will be pestering parents to buy the overpriced Apple for the home.

But even this is changing. No matter how much they love their children, most parents simply do not *have* the $2,500 to $3,500 necessary for a home Apple. The writers of educational software are realizing that if they write programs for more popular machines, they will sell more programs. (Since 1977, Apple has sold about 750,000 Apple IIs. In one year, Commodore has sold more than 1,000,000 VIC-20s. Further, many of the Apples IIs are being used in business, whereas almost all of the VIC-20s are in the home. If you were writing an educational program today, which would you choose?)

When you compare the basic Apple IIe unit ($1,395) with the Commodore 64 ($599 and falling) and the Atari 1200XL ($799, or less, depending on rebate), you'll see that Apple could obviously afford to sell the IIe for a lot less.

Put simply, Apple is overcharging each buyer of an Apple IIe by about $800. With Apple churning out IIes at the rate of one every thirty seconds, that comes to $96,000 of overcharging per hour. $768,000 per 8-hour day. No wonder Apple announced its quarterly profits were up by 73%.

The Lisa was named after the illegitimate daughter of Apple founder and chairman, Stephen Jobs. It was one of those macho, in-house, locker-room jokes that, unfortunately, stuck.

The Lisa was, uh, copied from Xerox. In December of 1979, Jobs attended a demonstration of Xerox's Smalltalk system. The demonstration was given by Xerox researcher Bruce Daniels. Six months later, Daniels (along with twenty-or-so other Xerox Smalltalk researchers) was working for the Lisa team at Apple. (Apple later decided it would be best to avoid an extended legal battle and now pays Xerox a licensing fee.)

The point most people seem to forget about the Lisa is that it costs $9,995. Do *you* have $9,995 to spend on a computer? I don't. And yet, I have never seen a consumer product selling for $9,995 get so much popular press. Major articles have appeared in *Time, Newsweek, The New York Times* and newspapers and magazines across the country.

Of course, Apple doesn't plan to sell the Lisa to you and me. They plan to sell it to managers, middle managers, upper middle managers, senior upper middle managers and other titled gentry along the corporate pathway. These movers and shakers, to whom $9,995 is but a requisition away, number, according to Apple, 30,000,000. (Heaven

"Oh, I don't know. I was thinking more along the lines of an IBM myself."

Of course, Apples are not for everyone.

"I will not buy an Apple, and get the hell out of here."

knows where they came up with *that* figure. It seems high to me. But, as you may have noted, *all* figures around Apple seem high to me.)

The Lisa uses a device known as a mouse to move a pointer around the screen. A mouse is a sort of executive joy stick. If you want to discard something, you move the pointer to a picture of a little garbage can and push a button. If you want to file something, you move the pointer to a picture of a little file folder and push a button. Business, then, becomes a computer game.

Although computer writers everywhere have hailed this system as the greatest thing since canned bananas, very few have asked, "Do we really *need* an executive business game?" and, more importantly, "Do executives really want to *play* computer games?"

These little pictures and the other graphics that make up the Lisa software take up a lot of memory (hence one reason for Lisa's high price tag), are difficult to program (Apple is fond of quoting how many man-centuries went into the development of the software), and may not be the most efficient method of handling information after all.

By comparison, an easy to learn and easy to use system is the Valdocs software that comes with the Epson QX-10. Here one's choices are presented in good old fashioned *words*. (The QX-10 is reviewed in detail later.)

For example, to get into the QX-10's telecommunications program, one simply pushes the MAIL button on the keyboard. One is presented with the message: "Please choose which mail function you wish to use and then press RETURN." The choices are: "Send Mail; Address Book; Person to person or network; Inbasket - Examine Log; or Outbasket - Examine Log." You can either push the first letter of your choice, or move the cursor to the first letter of your choice, and hit return. (Moving the cursor around the screen without a mouse! What will they think of next?)

With each of the choices come additional choices until the desired communication is sent, received, filed, displayed or discarded.

All of this is done from a keyboard, using cursor movement keys, and something we are already familiar

"Can't we even bring the Apple?"

with—words and letters. The Lisa requires, in addition to a keyboard, one square foot of desk space in which to manipulate the mouse. Do you know any busy person who has one square foot of empty space on his or her desk? I don't, especially after adding a computer and keyboard.

The price of the Epson QX-10, complete is $2,995. For the price of a Lisa you can buy three QX-10s, and have enough left over to buy three ColecoVisions for playing games.

The Lisa's software is tailor-made for the administrative executive. And that's about all it can do. Other software pickings range from slim to not. If executives buy Lisas in the same numbers that they bought Apple IIs with VisaCalc, Apple will have it made. If a high percentage these 30,000,000 executives don't, well, there's always new and bigger ad campaigns for the Apple IIe.

Some people may want a mouse and little pictures. Even there, the competition is offering a better value than the Lisa. In this, ironically, Apple may have planted the seeds of Lisa's—if not its own—destruction.

VisiCalc put Apple on the map. The electronic spreadsheet program was so spectacular that business people bought Apple IIs left and right because, at the time, Apple was the only computer VisiCalc would run on. Fade out 1978. Fade in 1982.

Apple, meanwhile, had developed their own electronic spreadsheet, which they began marketing in direct competition with VisiCalc. The VisiCalc ads showed a group of people peering into a computer, asking "What if...?" Apple went for the jugular. The headline of their ad campaign: "What if 'What if' Isn't Enough?" It was, to say the least, ungrateful.

1983: VisiCalc has announced a program, called VisiOn, which, they claim, will give an IBM Personal Computer 90% of the power of the Lisa for under $6,000, complete. Not only would one save money, one would have the flexibility and support of an IBM PC.

Meanwhile, the Apple polishers are saying, once again, wait. "Wait until later this year. Wait until Apple introduces the Mackintosh. It'll have all the power of the Lisa for $2,500. Just wait."

I'm waiting, I'm waiting.

Many people are devoted to their Apples. Here a group of Apple owners worship the tree from which they believe the first Apple fell.

If you have the time, of course, you can grow your own Apple.

Or you can climb a tree, go out on a limb, and pick one.

Franklin ACE 1000 and ACE 1200

The Franklin ACE 1000 keyboard includes a 12-key numeric pad, an alpha lock key and keys with special VisiCalc designations.

If for some reason you feel you *must* buy an Apple II for word processing, you might want to investigate the Franklin ACE 1000 or 1200.

The basic ACE costs about the same as the basic Apple IIe, but includes a better keyboard (although, like the Apple, it is not detachable), a numeric keypad, and 64K of RAM. All of the plug-in cards, programs, and peripherals made for the Apple will work with the Franklin ACE.

The ACE is better suited to word processing than the Apple IIe. The ACE 1000, however, requires the plug-in card for 80-column (like the Apple II, the standard is 40).

The ACE 1000 is in fact so close to the Apple II that Apple is suing ACE. (Apple seems to be suing *everyone* these days. Why don't they come out with a line of great new computers and let everyone else imitate their dust? As it stands they're trying to get universal proprietary rights on 1977 technology. Why?)

I don't think the ACE 1000 is a great value in computers if all you want to do is word processing. However, if for some reason you feel you *must* buy an Apple IIe for word processing...

The Franklin Computer Corporation, has introduced a new computer, the Franklin Ace 1200, that is both Apple-compatible *and* CP/M-compatible.

The 1200 is like the 1000 but has an 80-column

display, a Z-80 (CP/M) processor, 64K more memory, and both serial and parallel printer ports. The 1200 and the 1000 now have color capabilities built in.

The price is $2,495, which seems a bit high, but is less than a comparably equipped Apple. So, if you need to use one or more Apple programs, and still want to do some serious word processing or business applications, you might want to look at an ACE 1200.

Commodore

Commodore makes an amazing — if not confusing — array of computers. Try as I might, I have not been able to find one that I can recommend as a word processor.

The VIC-20 is a great value in small, introductory computers. (At $300 it's a much better buy than Radio Shack's Color Computer and, for many, better than the Atari 400 or 800.) But the 22 character lines, the fact that the screen display is not terribly sharp, the fact that there is not powerful word processing software available, etc. etc. would put it in the Atari category of word processing.

The PET has only 40 characters per line, hence the drawbacks of the Apple apply.

The 8032, or CBM — Commodore Business Machine — is best suited to word processing. The problem is that it is not a CP/M based machine and therefore one is locked into the Commodore software. At the present this does not include a spell-check program. Further, the keyboard is not detachable.

The Commodore 64 is a CP/M machine, but, again, has only 40 characters per line. Sigh.

Commodore seems to be after the Apple/Atari market at the moment. Their computers, advertising and pricing reflect this, and they seem to be doing a good job of it. When they decide to go after the IBM/Xerox market, then Commodore will be in the word processing business.

Heath/Zenith

The Heath H-89 is not the greatest personal computer in the world, but it's not bad. For word processing, it is better than the Apple IIe or TRS-80 III or Atari in almost all ways. The screen display is a full 24 80-character lines. It has not one but two Z-80 microprocessors. It is CP/M based. It has an 80 character keyboard with a numeric keypad. It offers both WordStar and PeachText, available directly from Heath. Not bad.

The drawbacks of the Heath H-89 with regard to word processing are: The keyboard is not detachable. The video display is not the world's sharpest. It has but one disk drive although more can be added.

The H-89 has one advantage that no other full-size personal computer offers: It comes in a kit form and you put it together yourself. This may not seem like much of an advantage, but putting together one's personal computer personally can be surprisingly enjoyable. (Assembled, the H-89 is distributed by Zenith as the Z-89. The H-89 sells for $1,895, the Z-89 for $2,895.)

I would think that the H-89 would be a fine word processor for someone who wanted to learn about computers from the inside out on a limited budget.

The Osborne 1

The actual size of the Osborne 1 screen

The Osborne 1 is a funny computer, as fascinating and idiosyncratic as the man who designed it, Adam Osborne. Adam Osborne wrote about computers until he finally decided he could do a better job of computer manufacturing than the companies he was writing about, so he formed Osborne Computer Company and the rest is recent history.

The main advantages of the Osborne 1 are price and portability.

For $1,795 you get a computer with 64K of RAM, video display, two disk drives (92K capacity per drive), a semidetachable keyboard with numeric keypad, a Z-80 microprocessor and enough programs to open your own software store. You get CP/M, WordStar, MailMerge, SuperCalc (an electronic spreadsheet program), and not one but two BASIC programs, MBASIC (Microsoft Basic) and CBASIC.

All this fits into a 23.5-pound package that is portable — not portable like a calculator is portable, but portable like a portable sewing machine is portable. Portable or not, in the

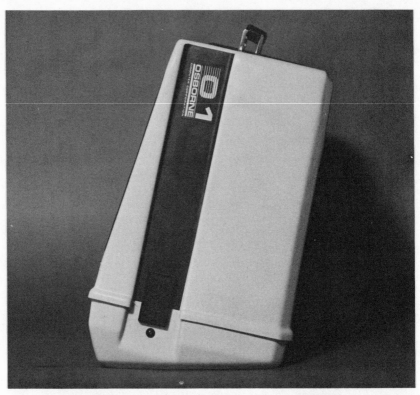

Folded, the Osborne 1 resembles a tipsy sewing machine

The new version of the Osborne 1, unfolded

world of personal computers, it is an unbelievable value.

The keyboard is good. It has a numeric keypad, ten programmable function keys and separate cursor movement keys that work with WordStar.

The Osborne 1, alas, has a tragic flaw. It can be summed up in three words: The Video Display. The built-in video screen has a diagonal measurement that is slightly smaller than five inches.

The screen displays 24 lines of text, but each line is only 52 characters long. This is barely acceptable for word processing. An external video monitor enlarges the size of the screen to a "regulation" twelve inches, but the 52-character line length remains. When blown up on the larger video screen, the characters are readable but not too sharp.

Osborne Executive

Contrary to popular belief, the next Osborne computer will not be the Osborne II, it will not have a 9-inch screen, and it will not cost less than the Osborne 1. So much for rumors.

The screen on the Osborne Executive will be—are you ready—seven inches. In a phrase, this simply will not do. On an 80-column line, the letters are not perceptibly larger than on the 52-column line of the Osborne 1 5-inch screen.

When this "New! Larger! All-Our-Former-Problems-Are-Solved!" screen appears, a good number of people will believe that larger screen size equals larger and easier to read letters. It will not. It *cannot*.

A bit of math here: Increasing the screen size from 5 inches to 7 inches slightly more than doubles the useable screen area (from 12 square inches to 24.75 square inches of screen area). You can bet the ads will read, "The New Osborne Screen is MORE THAN TWICE AS BIG as our old screen!" This means that, if Osborne kept the 52-characters-per-line he now has, each character would be twice as large.

However, (our math continues) Osborne plans to increase his line length from 52-columns to 80-columns, an increase of 65%. So, he will be increasing his screen area by 106%, but will also be increasing the information on that screen by 65%, which means the total increase in character size can only be 41%.

I am sure that we will not be seeing ads proclaiming, "The Characters Are Now Not Quite Half Again as Large!" Considering the smallness of the letters to begin with, an increase of 41% will be a help, but not really a solution.

I don't know why Osborne didn't go to a full 9-inch screen (the minimum, in my estimation, for comfortable computing). I also don't know why he's taken this long to enlarge his screen at all. Maybe, after all this time, a 9-inch screen would be like admitting, "I've been wrong all this time after all." (The Osborne position is that no one really *needs* a screen larger than 5-inches. In the Osborne Cosmology, larger screens are a frivolous waste of phosphor.)

Whatever the reasons, 7-inches is not going to make it. (See the review of the Zorba later on.) Sorry, Adam.

The Osborne Executive has 128K of RAM, 182K per disk drive, and retails for $2,495.

Photo: John C. Dvorak

Adam Osborne explaining that, according to his survey, there is "little perceptual difference" between 7 and 9 inches. Adam apparently did not ask Eve.

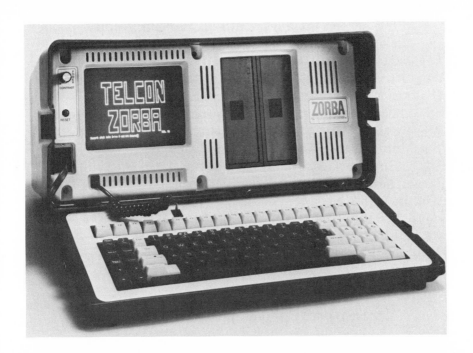

The Zorba

The Zorba is a fine little computer with one tragic flaw. I'll tell you the flaw before telling you the good stuff so you won't think I'm leading you on.

The screen is too small. It's a 7-inch screen, and the letters are simply too small to work with comfortably for a long period of time. The letters are crisp and sharp and fully-formed, but they're too small for everyday use. (This is my decision. Please have a look for yourself.)

One of the nicest features of the Zorba is that it can emulate several popular disk formats. It will actually read and write disks in various formats. This makes the Zorba an excellent second computer if you have one of the computers that it emulates. (When used occasionally while traveling, the small screen size is less of a distraction.) (Note that some programs require a special *terminal* as well as disk format. The Zorba may or may not be compatible with your terminal, even if it is compatible with the disk drives. Check carefully before deciding to buy.)

The screen displays a full 25 80-column lines. It has two disk drives, each holding 400K of information. The keyboard is detachable, has a numeric keypad, separate cursor movement keys, and 19 programmable function keys that are easily programmed.

The price is $1,995, which includes WordStar, Mail-Merge, CalcStar, CBASIC, M80, and CP/M. Nice price, nice machine, small screen.

But wait! Could that light at the end of the tunnel be a larger screen? Yes, it is! Coming soon, as they say, is the Nomis, from the same people who make the Zorba. (Where *do* they get their names?) The Nomis is like the Zorba, but it has a 9-inch screen and 800K per drive. The price is $2,395. Will the 10 magabyte KayPro 10 at $2,795 steal Nomis's thunder. Tune in again for tomorrow's episode of "As The Disk Turns."

KAYPRO II (Formerly KAYCOMP II)

My review of the Osborne 1 in *Popular Computing* included the following:

It's easy to speculate on how the Osborne 1 *might* have been designed to hold a larger screen. First, the various input/output ports could have been placed at the rear of the machine...This would have removed the ports from the front panel, where they are generally a nuisance. With a modem, a printer, an IEEE-488 peripheral, and the keyboard all attached to the computer by means of wide, flat cable, approaching the disk drive is almost as difficult as mating with a reluctant octopus.

Next, the disks could have been mounted horizontally and placed beside each other, leaving room for a 7-or 8-inch video monitor.

Well, the KayPro people moved the input/output ports to the rear, mounted their drives not horizontally but vertically, and made room for not a 7-or 8-inch but a *nine-*inch monitor. This allows for a full 24 lines with 80

characters per line. The screen is green phosphor. (The Osborne is black & white.)

The screen is more readable than the Osborne, even with the Osborne 12-inch video monitor attached.

The keyboard of the KayPro II is excellent. It has a detachable keyboard with six feet of coiled cable. The KayPro II weighs about two pounds more than the Osborne 1.

The two built-in disk drives each hold 191K of information (compared with Osborne's 92). 64K of memory is standard (same as Osborne).

The case is metal, as opposed to Osborne's molded plastic. (The new Osborne case looks more sophisticated, although the KayPro II has an attractive "high tech" look. When standing on end the KayPro II is not tipsy. Certainly metal is more rugged than plastic.)

Put simply, the KayPro II is — in terms of hardware — equal to or better than one of the greatest computer success stories of modern times, the Osborne 1. Its cost? The same as the Osborne 1, $1,795. (What a coincidence, hey?)

The KayPro II, like the Osborne 1, offers a small software store free with purchase. CP/M, MBASIC, Profit Plan (an electronic spreadsheet), and the entire line of Perfect software. ("Perfect" is a trade name, not necessarily a product description.) This includes Perfect Writer (reviewed earlier), Perfect Filer, Perfect Calc (yet another electronic spreadsheet), and Perfect Speller.

The weak link in the Perfect chain is Perfect Speller. It checks for root words and then adds prefixes and suffixes to them. This means that not-real words, made up of acceptable prefixes, acceptable suffixes, and acceptable root words, could slip by. "Thoughful" for "thoughtful," "verbage" for "verbiage," or "courtious" for "courteous," might not be tagged for correction. Given the state-of-the-art of spell check programs, this is unacceptable. To shore up this weak link, KayPro gives away The Word Plus with each KayPro— the best spell-check program around.

I am pleased with the way the KayPro people respond to the comments of the marketplace. Criticized by some for the word processing program they once offered (Select), KayPro offered another (Perfect Writer). I am pleased, too, with the support the Kaypro people are giving those who have already purchased the Kaypro II. For only $75, current owners of the KayPro II can add the entire collection of Perfect software to their machines. (A retail value of almost $1,000!)

This is certainly the most impressive array of free-with-purchase software included with any machine at any price.

I think of the KayPro like the VW beetle back in the 1960s: cheap, reliable transportation; ugly, but it grows on you. It is not, however, a Cadillac, or a Mercedes, but then, not everyone can afford, and some might not even want, a Cadillac or a Mercedes. It's nice to have the KayPro II available in the market place. When compared with, say, an Osborne or an Apple, it is a far better word processor and a far better buy. I use my KayPro II when I'm on the road, and like it. I do not, however, use it at home.

If you need word processing and can't afford more, or if you need portability, the KayPro II is an excellent choice.

If you can afford more, and you don't need portability, look carefully at the Epson QX-10, TeleVideo 803 (both reviewed later) or any of the other highly-rated computers in this book (IBM, Rainbow, Decmate II, etc.).

Yes, the economical computer of choice is the KayPro II. Matched with the Smith-Corona TP-1, it gives you a great word processor for less than $2,500.

KayPro 10

The KayPro 10 is very much like the KayPro II (what happened to the seven computers in between?) except that the KayPro 10 has only one floppy disk drive and a built-in 10 megabyte hard disk. KayPro continues to astound one with the price: $2,795. (Some 10 megabyte disks *alone* cost more than $3,000.) Amazing.

The machine is wonderful, a superb value, and all that, but I have one major concern: the hard disk. In the world of personal computers, hard disks are considered delicate beasties, who must be treated gently, and with the respect that's due anything that can destroy on whim 5,000 typewritten pages of information.

When a hard disk is put in a *portable* computer, considering the knocks and bangs portable anythings are subjected to, I become worried.

The KayPro people assure me that the disk drive is of a new design and double shock mounted and on and on. I still keep thinking about 5,000 typewritten pages being wiped out by one careless porter.

Of course, as with any hard disk computer, one should back up information on a regular basis. This is good advice, and like all good advice, seldom taken. A 10 megabyte hard disk holds the same amount of information as *fifty* 200K KayPro floppy disks.

Granted, one will seldom have 10 full megabytes of information that will need frequent backing up. Much of the disk will be empty, or filled with programs that are already on master disks somewhere. But, still, the idea of making even 20 backup disks on a regular basis is, well, not appealing.

Please understand that these are subjective, primordial, emotional reactions, like the fear of flying. (99.9999% of all airline flights are completed safely. 50,000 more people die in traffic accidents every year than in plane crashes. Then why am I afraid of going on an airplane and not afraid when I get behind the wheel of my car? It's not logical, especially the way I drive, but there it is.) I wanted to share all this with you, doctor, so that I could get it all into the open, talk about it, maybe get over some of this fear.

You see, the KayPro 10 is a great computer. It's fast, has a nice screen display (better than its little brother), has an attractive blue-grey brushed metal case, has all the software given with the KayPro II. And it's the best hard disk computer bargain around.

This computer is heaven-sent for people with tens of thousands of things to file. The titles of whole *libraries* or bookstores or auto parts companies or baseball card collections can be put on this computer.

Ten magabytes could handle the accounting, inventory, and word processing needs of a good-sized company, and still leave room for the boss's computer games.

Then why am I afraid? Why do I fear the letter that says: "I took your advice and I bought this thing and after five months of putting everything I know on it it broke and I hate you forever.?"

Ten magabytes is a lot. It's very powerful, but very dangerous. *Please*, with this or any other hard disk computer, *back up your irreplaceable information regularly*. Back-up information is like wearing a seat belt: If it's only used once in ten years, it was worth the effort.

Maybe the KayPro 10 and I should get away somewhere, take a long trip together or something, and maybe we can work on my anxiety together.

Otrona Attache

The Otrona Attache is a portable personal computer that begins to approach true portability. It weighs eighteen pounds — five pounds less than the Osborne. The Attache is also smaller and more compact.

The screen size of the Attache is the same five inches as the Osborne, but the display is a full 24 eighty-character lines. Because the Otrona uses a high-resolution screen, each character is sharper than on the Osborne. Further, the screen is capable of high-quality graphics, something the Osborne is not.

Two 5¼-inch disk drives are built in, each drive holding 380K of storage, more than four times the Osborne's capacity.

And the price for all these wonders? You guessed it, more than twice as much as the Osborne, $3,995. That price includes CP/M, WordStar, Microsoft Basic, and a graphics package. It does not include MailMerge, CBASIC, or Super-Calc, which the Osborne does.

The Attache keyboard is truly detachable. It uses standard coiled telephone cable (the kind that goes between the handset and the phone), so a 25-foot extension cable can be purchased at your local Phone Store for $9.95. The keyboard is full-size and responsive. The numeric keypad has been omitted due to space limitations, a wise choice.

The cursor keys move the cursor around in WordStar, and the keyboard has several of the most commonly used WordStar commands assigned to clearly labeled keys on the top row. This would allow one not familiar with WordStar to perform basic editing functions with very little training.

For larger screen display the Otrona will plug into any video monitor.

Escort

A few years ago I started a publishing company. I called it Lion Press because lions were my favorite animals and I had a mane of hair that made me look like a character out of *The Wizard of Oz*.

I commissioned my favorite cartoonist, Charles Addams, to draw the colophon (trademark). I asked him to revise a *New Yorker* cover he had drawn in which a lion was pointing to a chart depicting the hierarchy of the animal kingdom with, naturally, the lion at the top.

I requested that, rather than ordinary animals, the chart include the colophons — especially the animal colophons — of all the other publishers: Bantam's rooster, Penguin's penguin, Pocket Book's kangaroo, Knopf's dog — even Simon & Schuster's human.

Proudly I took out ads in *Publishers Weekly* announcing my new company and our Charles Addams colophon. Stationery was printed, business cards, envelopes, and 20,000 copies of our first book. Like falling in love, it was expensive, but worth it.

Then one day I came home to find a message on my service: Mr. Ross from Lion Books had called. From Lion Books? But *I* was Lion Books; Lion Press, actually, but it was the same thing.

I called Mr. Ross, who kindly explained to me that

LEO PRESS

12/31/75

he too thought there was little difference between Lion Books and Lion Press. He, however, had started Lion Books ten years before.

We agreed that there was only room in the publishing jungle for one Lion. I asked him if he would like a good buy on a colophon and some beautiful stationery.

I empathize, then, with Jonos Ltd., makers of the Courier Portable Computer. After ads and circulars and operating manuals and stationery, ITT contacted Jonos and let them know that ITT was already making a computer product, a terminal, known as the Courier.

Jonas decided that one might be able to fight City Hall, but not ITT. (The ITT person who contacted them had the title "Senior Staff Trademark Counsel." How would you like to fight a trademark infringement case against a company that had a Senior Staff Trademark Counsel?)

Jonos renamed their computer. It's now called the Escort.

The Escort combines the portability of the Attache with the large (9-inch) screen of the KayPro II. It does this by using the Sony 3½-inch MicroFloppy disk drives. These take up less room (and have less weight) than 5¼-inch drives. Two are built into the Escort (with a generous 322K per drive).

The Escort costs the same as the Otrona, $3,995. That price includes CP/M, Spellbinder (word processing), Spellguard (spell checking) Multiplan (electronic worksheet), and Microsoft BASIC.

If it's portability you're after, be sure to compare the Otrona Attache with the Escort and see which one you prefer.

In the meanwhile, the Escort people spend each day hoping the Senior Staff Trademark Counsel from Ford Motor Company does not get in touch, just as we at Prelude Press fear that long-overdue call from Honda.

Sony Typecorder

    While on the subject of portability, I thought I would mention the Sony Typecorder. The Typecorder is not a personal computer. It will not run programs. It has no video screen or disk drives. It is, however a highly portable word recorder.

    The name Typecorder is descriptive. It has a tape recorder that will record dictation on a microcassette. It also has a typewriter keyboard that will record words on the same microcassette. The whole thing is the size of an 8½ x 11 sheet of paper, is 1½ inches thick and weighs three pounds. It costs $1,500.

    Words are typed into the standard QWERTY keyboard and displayed on a single-line, forty-character liquid crystal display, the same sort of display most hand-held calculators currently use. Forty characters is about half a line, and after a full line a carriage return must be hit. (No word wrap on the Typecorder.) About 50 pages of text can be stored on the microcassette. The microcassette can then be turned over for the storage of another fifty.

You can scroll forward or backward in the text, making changes as you go. As you can imagine, having one-half line displayed at any one time severely limits editing. The battery lasts more than five hours, long enough for a cross-country flight.

The text can then be transferred to your personal computer through an optional communication package. Here it can be edited using whatever word processing software you have. The microcassette can also fit directly into the Sony word processor, a stand alone word processor that is nice but, at $10,000, a bit expensive. If you have unlimited funds, however...

The Typecorder itself is $695. If you are addicted to recording your words through a keyboard, as I seem to be, and if you spend a great deal of time on airplanes or commuter trains or in the High Sierras backpacking, the Sony Typecorder might prove an excellent addition to whichever word processing computer you select.

Epson HX-20

In the world of truly portable word recorders, one must certainly include the Epson HX-20. The Epson includes a full keyboard (better than the Typecorder), a 20-character four-line screen, and a built-in 20-column dot matrix printer. The price is $795. A microcassette can be added for around $135. The batteries of the HX-20 last a remarkable 50 hours. Recharging time is 8 hours.

The folks at Roger Hagan Associates are selling a $65 program that will allow the HX-20 to record words just fine. It's called Wordproc. They are quite honest about the limitations of the program and about the HX-20 as a word processor. But the advantages of the HX-20 (or the Type-corder) as a word recorder are many. Roger Hagan Associates' address is at the end of the Book.

The Teleram T-3000

Where do companies get their numbers from? I mean, what connection does the number "3000" have with this computer? I can't figure it out. I imagine a group of Vice Presidents in Charge of Product Naming were sitting around one day, and one said, "What shall we call this thing?"

Another said, "How about the Teleram 1?"

"No," another said, "Osborne already has the Osborne 1."

"Well, how about the Teleram II? It has a nice alliterative quality."

"I don't think so. There's already a KayPro II, and a *Superman II*, and *Tea for Two*."

"Teleram III?"

"Apple III, *Three's Company*..."

"Let's tie it to the machine somehow. What does it weigh?"

"About nine pounds."

"How about the Teleram Nine?"

"No. Ice-Nine, *Plan Nine from Outer Space*. Besides, *nein* is 'no' in German. 'Teleram' is a German Sounding name, like Telefunken. We don't want anyone to think the Germans said 'no' to this product.

"Well, what does the thing cost?"

"Oh, around $3,000."

"That's it! The Teleram 3000!"

A quick check of all known products, movies, television shows, and song titles revealed that nothing had ever been named 3000 before.

"It's good. It's very good," said the head of the Product Naming Division, who up until this time had been silent. "But we need a zinger, a grabber...an alliteration, a rhyme..." He drew deep within himself, lost for a moment in creative thought.

The room was so still you could hear a microchip counting.

The head of the Product Naming Division returned from his reverie. "The Teleram T-3000," he announced.

"Brilliant, J.B.!"

"Superb!"

"Incredible!"

"It has alliteration. It has rhyme. You're a genius, J.B."

J.B. looked at the floor and shuffled his feet. "I just do my job the best I can," he said, and the Teleram T-3000 was born.

I don't mean to pick on Teleram. The same is true of almost any numbered computer (or any numbered consumer product): What on earth do those numbers have to do with reality? Who makes them up? Do they get paid? Does it add a nickel to the cost of everything we buy? I wish Ralph Nader would investigate this one.

The Teleram T-3000 (hereinafter referred to as the Teleram) is the most portable full-function computer available. It's perfect for people who travel a lot on planes or commuter trains. (I assume anyone who can afford that many plane tickets or a house in the country can afford a $2,995 computer.)

The Teleram weighs about nine pounds, has a full-function keyboard, and four eighty-character lines of display. The display is liquid crystal, like pocket calculators. While one would not want to write a magnum opus on a four line screen, it's surprisingly useable — far more so than the one-half line displays found in other portables.

The Teleram stores information on a bubble memory. Bubble memory is user-changeable, like RAM, but it keeps the information indefinitely, even when the power is turned off, like ROM. It's a great combination of the two, but, at the moment, fairly expensive. The $2,995 price includes 128K of bubble memory. An additional 128K is $600.

128K is usually more than sufficient. A word processing program might take half of it (Wordstar, for example, consumes 68K), which would leave about 60K (30 double-spaced typewritten pages) for files. After a journey, the document files would be transferred to disks, and the memory erased, leaving 60K again for the next trip.

The batteries of the Teleram last about five hours before recharging. In the near future, an interface unit, disk drives, and a video monitor will be available. This would allow the Teleram to be used as a regular computer in the home or office, and a portable computer on the road.

The Teleram will also plug into any computer, and data can be transferred to or from the Teleram.

Teleram is best known for its portable workstations used by journalists throughout the country. If they can build reliable terminals that hold up to the daily grind of on-the-road reporters, you can bet they have the technology to make a reliable portable computer.

Morrow Micro Decision

This is a fine computer and an excellent value. In terms of overall value it runs neck and neck with the KayPro II. The Morrow has a larger screen than the Kay-Pro II, but it costs a bit more and it's not portable.

The standard Morrow Micro Decision computer comes with one disk drive (186K formatted capacity); a 12-inch green phosphor screen (25 80-character lines); a Z80A processor; 64K of RAM; a detachable keyboard with a numeric keypad, separate cursor movement keys, and seven programmable function keys.

And that's not all: Morrow is a member-in-good-standing of the Great Software Giveaway Program. You

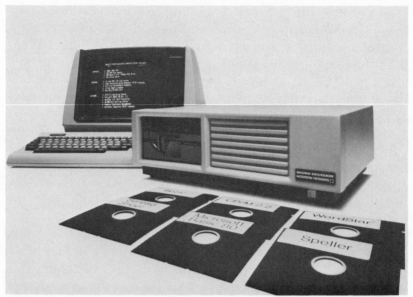

get, free with purchase, CP/M, Pilot (a program that makes CP/M more friendly), WordStar, Microsoft BASIC (MBASIC), BaZic (for NorthStar compatibility), Correct-It (a spell-check program), and LogiCalc (an electronic spreadsheet).

All this for $1,590. One more 186K disk drive (highly recommended) brings the price to $1,940.

The screen display is sharp, clear, and legible. (On the prototype monitor I saw, the lines undulated ever so slightly. I'm hoping this will be corrected in production units.) The keyboard is solid, with a good feel. My only complaint, as a user, is the noise the disk drives make. Sometimes they sound like a subway braking, and at other times they sound like Darth Vadar breathing. I'm hoping that (A) the noises were only in the drives I listened to, or (B) not everyone is as delicate about the sound of disk drives as I am.

I first heard about the Morrow Micro Decision the way I hear about most things these days: a letter from a reader. This reader wrote:

"The company is MORROW DESIGNS out of San Leandro (California) and seems to be a well established producer of hard disks and S-100 type board components.

DUN'S Directory tells me they have thirty-five employees and the listed officers are all named Morrow. I have traced their ads back to 1979."

I do believe I have the most wonderful readers in the world. I wrote back and told him he should consider working for *Sixty Minutes*.

I do not know how many employees Morrow has (I do know the boss is named Mr. Morrow), but I know they have a good reputation and have been around the computer world longer than I have. They are a solid company, and will no doubt stand behind their product.

However, it is a new computer, and the precautions that apply to any new computer do apply. As Fats Waller said more than once, "One never knows, do one?"

The Morrow Micro Decision is a great computer at a great price, and well worth your consideration.

Sanyo MBC 1000

The Sanyo is also a good computer at a fair price. It is similar to the Morrow, except whereas Morrow gives extra software, Sanyo gives extra disk capacity. (186K per drive on the Morrow, 326K per drive on the Sanyo.)

The basic Sanyo includes one disk drive (326K); a 12-inch green phosphor screen (25 80-character lines); 64K of RAM; and a detachable keyboard with separate cursor movement keys, numeric keypad, and five function keys. Also included is CP/M and SBASICII.

The price is $1,995. An additional disk drive is $695. (The extra disk sits in its own cabinet off to one side.) This would bring the price of a two-drive system to $2,690. All you'd have to add is a word processing program and a printer.

The weak link of the Sanyo is the screen display. The characters are formed using only a 6x7 dot resolution, and the dots are therefore noticeable. The display, however, is far from intolerable, and better than, say, Apple II or Radio Shack III. (But not as good as Morrow.)

The Sanyo is likely to be sold in a bundled package — computer, printer, software, everything — for one price.

Cromemco C-10

Configured for word processing, the Cromemco offers a keyboard, monochrome (green) video screen, Z80 processor, 64K of memory, two 390K 5¼-inch disk drives, a "CP/M-compatible" operating system, a word processing program, a spreadsheet program, and a structured BASIC program. All this will cost you $2,380.

If you'd like to economize, you can leave off one of the disk drives, and the entire package would cost $1,785. A second disk drive can be added later for $595.

The keyboard, although detachable, is small and does not include a numeric keypad. The programs are Cromemco's Own. I have not had a chance to use them, so I cannot comment on them. Since they come free with a computer that is a good buy even without software, if the software doesn't meet your needs, you can always buy a program that does.

Although this is a new computer, Cromemco has been making small computers for some time. Let's hope the bugs that so often plague new computers have been worked out in design and testing, and not in the marketplace. (This hope, disclaimer, and warning are true of *all* newly introduced computers.)

This is a good, economical, and welcome addition to the world of personal computing.

Toshiba T100

A Toshiba personal computer, configured for word processing, would include a full-function keyboard, a mono-chrome (green) screen, Z80 processor, 64K of memory, two 280K 5¼-inch disk drives, and CP/M. All this for $2,380.

The weak link in this system is the video display. Although an 8x8 dot-matrix character generation should be adequate, for some reason the letters look broken and spotty. This could just be the display of the unit I saw, or it might be inherent in the design. I would recommend comparing the video display quality with other comparably priced personal computers before you buy.

A positive aspect of the video display is that, with the simple addition of a color monitor, the T100 is capable of full-color graphic display.

The Eagle II

There is lots of good news and one piece of bad news about the Eagle II computer. First, the good news:

It has a good keyboard, fine screen, Z80 processor, 64K of memory, two 390K 5¼-inch disk drives, and costs but $2,995. More good news: The $2,995 price also includes CP/M, CBASIC, UltraCalc spreadsheet, and the Spellbinder word processing program.

A great buy, that. And now for the bad news: It does not have a detachable keyboard. To quote Charlie Brown, "Arghhhh!"

A detachable keyboard? I'll give you a detachable keyboard.

NorthStar Advantage

NorthStar has been making computers for a number of years, their Horizon being one of the most respected and dependable ever made.The Advantage is NorthStar's first "all-in-one" computer. (The Horizon requires the addition of a terminal.) They have made a fine machine, reasonably priced (around $4,000). Unfortunately they took the concept of all-in-one a bit too far: The keyboard is not detachable. For reasons detailed in the last chapter, a nondetachable keyboard is a major drawback in word processing applications.

The Advantage has one advantage: It does high-quality computer graphics. Any business that needs graphics *and* word processing would do well to consider the Advantage.

TeleVideo 802

TeleVideo is one of the foremost manufacturers of inexpensive, high quality video terminals. In 1981 they introduced several personal and business computers, and the 802 is the latest addition to that line.

It's a fine computer and a good value. They took their popular top-of-the-line 950 terminal and added 64K of memory, a Z-80 processor and two disk drives with 340K per drive. With a CP/M operating system included, the retail price is $3,495. Discounts are frequently available.

The keyboard is detachable, and the screen display is one of the best. There are 24 eighty-character lines, numeric keypad, cursor movement keys, and 22 programmable function keys. The keyboard and screen are state-of-the-art all the way.

The major problem with the TeleVideo 802 is that it is not distributed as widely as some of the other computers discussed in this section. Therefore, finding a neighborhood store with 802 experts might be difficult. Let's hope this situation improves over time.

Televideo TS803

The "TS" in "TS803" stands for, I think, Tres Sexy. This latest computer from TeleVideo is the sexiest thing this side of Euphoria.

The design is, how you say, ooh-lah-lah. If this computer does not win some design award somewhere, there is no justice. Aesthetics aside, the 803 is a powerful, full-featured computer at a great price ($2,495).

TeleVideo, more than any company I know, has no fear of making the computer they introduced only a few months before nearly obsolete by the introduction of a totally new computer.

They began with the 801, which basically added a processor, memory and two disk drives to their already popular 950 terminal. In its day (a year ago) it was a good value. Then came the 802, which housed all the personal computer elements in one sleek package. Suddenly the 801 seemed a bit clunky.

Now, with the 803, which looks as though it were designed by Maserati, with more features, and a full $1,000 less than the 802, well, is there any doubt which consumers will choose?

The 803 is an 8-bit Z80 computer, with 64K of RAM (expandable to 128K). For those of you who may some day want to attach a rodent to your computer, there is a mouse port built in. The CP/M operating system is included in the price.

The two disk drives each hold (get this) 368.6K of information. (That's what the specifications say. Nothing like being precise. That .6K—about 75 words—may come in handy some day.)

The screen is green-phosphor and measures not 12, but 14 inches. (Does this mark the beginning of a size war among manufacturers?) The screen tilts up and down.

The keyboard has every key imaginable, plus sixteen special function keys, labeled word processing keys, and a numeric keypad. The TeleVideo has made some of my favorite keyboards, and this one is no exception. The keyboard is detachable, of course, and has a long cord.

Rather than end suddenly below the space bar, like most keyboards, this one slants gradually down, providing a place for a typist to rest the heels of the hands. As with most design innovations, some people will like this, others won't, and most people won't notice.

There is no fan, so the unit is quiet, silent in fact. For those deep thinkers who prefer creation without the whir of white noise, this machine is certainly worth listening to.

Although on the whole I am enthusiastic about the TeleVideo 803, I have a few reservations. Although the silence of no fan is nice, the disk drives, when they operate, sound a bit like muffled coffee grinders, and not the sort that Bessie Smith sang about. This is a minor distraction, as the disks seldom turn when any "serious" computer input is going on.

Also, the 803 has a slight electronic click each time a key is hit. Some people, especially touch typists, like this. The 802 has a switch in the back to turn the keyclick off, but I could find no such switch on the back of the 803. I'm sure that some technical type somewhere knows how to turn it off.

While I find the larger letters on the 14-inch screen easier to work with, they don't seem to have the sharpness of the 802; it's easier to see the little dots that make up each letter. A check of the specifications shows why. The 802 has a character resolution of 10x14 with a 7x10 dot matrix, while the 803 has an 8x10 resolution with a 7x9 dot matrix.

The decreases are not significant, but, when combined with the larger character size on the screen, the degeneration of character quality is noticeable. I should point out that the screen display is perfectly readable, and anyone who did not have the 802 display to compare it with would probably never know that a dot here and a dot there were missing.

These few cavils should, however, be considered minor complaints, especially when the price of the unit, $2,495, is taken into account. The only competition TeleVideo has in that price range and in a full-size, full-function personal computer that would lend itself well to business and word processing, is the Epson QX-10.

The TS803 is a new product, and so I will give my standard New Product Warning: Any new machine as complex as a personal computer may have bugs, so beware. That applies to all new computers, or new models of old computers. I'm not anticipating difficulty with the 803 (which is TeleVideo's third generation of personal computers), but if you want a fully debugged unit, you might want to consider the TeleVideo 802. It's a fine machine, every bit as powerful as the 803, and my guess is, with the 803 now on the scene, there should be some good buys on 802s.

Xerox 820-II

The Xerox 820-II is the revised version of the Xerox 820. It has a detachable keyboard with numeric keypad and separate cursor keys, black and white video display (24 80-character lines), 64K of RAM, and a Z80A processor. This basic unit costs $2,245.

Disk drives can them be added in 5¼-inch, 8-inch, and hard disk formats. Two 5¼-inch drives, with 360K of storage per drive, run $1,450. CP/M is an additional $200.

This would put the price of a Xerox 820-II, configured like a TeleVideo 802, to $3,895.

Sales abound, however, in the Land of Xerox. Contact your local Xerox Store for the latest special.

Hewlett Packard HP 86 and HP 125

Hewlett Packard is one of the big names in the computer business. They cater to business, and this is reflected by their computers — and by their prices.

The top of the line "personal" computer is the HP 125. It has a good screen, good keyboard, two 5¼-inch drives (270K per drive), 64K of memory, a Z80 processor, and CP/M. As a personal computer to be used as a word processor, it meets all criteria except value: it's almost $5,000.

The HP 125 is not sold as a personal computer, however. It's official designation is "HP 125 Business Assistant." While $5,000 is too much to pay for a personal computer, $5,000 for a Business Assistant is *cheap*.

The personal personal computer is the HP 86. It seems more patched together than designed. The basic unit (keyboard, memory, and processor) is $1,795. 260K 5¼-inch disk drives are $850 *each*. And a monitor is $325. It is not a CP/M based machine, although I was told a plug-in module was available for an undisclosed amount.

This adds up to a machine with the appearance and capabilities of a Toshiba, but the price of a IBM.

When I voiced my concern about prices to the HP salespeople, I was told that these were only the retail

The HP 125

prices, and that dealers frequently sold the machines for much less.

That being the case, I would say that the HP 125 would make a good Word Processing Assistant if sold for $3,500 to $4,000.

The HP 86 would have to sell for about $2,500 — including the CP/M module — before it could successfully compete.

NEC APC

NEC, the people who make the finest letter-quality printer around, make several small computers marketed by at least two different divisions.

The one that seems to be getting the most attention is the APC, which stands for Advanced Personal Computer. As fond as I am of the NEC printers, I must admit I am not very fond of the APC.

The keyboard is solid, and the screen display is clear, but then so is the keyboard and screen display of computers costing half as much. The drives are 8-inch, and only 8-inch. They are also the noisiest drives I have heard on a small computer.

The processor is 16-bit. The software for the APC is limited, and there is no adapter card for running 8-bit software.

All this for $3,998. If it were $2,000 cheaper, it might be a breakthrough. As it is, it's not a great word processing value.

The strength of this machine seems to be when a color monitor is added. This is of little importance to a word processing computer, although a business that requires color graphics would appreciate the sharpness of the color display. (And if you're someone who *must* do word processing in color, this would be a machine to investigate.) (The color monitor adds about $1,000 to the price.)

At various points in this book when I recommend buying an NEC, please keep in mind that I am referring to the *Spinwriter Letter Quality Printer*, and not the Advanced Personal Computer.

Alas.

The Lanier TypeMaster

I know I said I wouldn't review stand alone word processors, but I think it's time for a little comic relief, brought to us by the people who brought us No Problem Typing: Lanier.

Before I tell you the amazing price, let me tell you what you get. You get a keyboard and a screen. So far so good. You get two disk drives with a whopping 70K per drive. You get software and a year's service contract.

And you get a printer — *built in.*

Yes, your paper goes in the top of the TypeMaster not unlike bread in a toaster. *I am not making this up.* There is really a printer built into this word processor. All-in-one has never been — and pray Heaven never again will be — taken this far.

The price for this desktop marvel? "We're having a Special this month. It's only around $7,000." The voice behind the Special Price was the Lanier salesperson, one of those salespeople who you don't just want to have an affair with: You want to get *married* and raise a *family.*

So, if you're tired of singles bars, in need of a good chuckle, have money to burn and bread to toast, visit your local Lanier office. Or just give them a call: they'll come to *you.*

(Be sure to ask about the TypeMaster with the built-in dishwasher, bottle opener, coffee maker, and pasta machine. It's on Special next month.)

IBM Personal Computer

I have said more than a few disparaging words about IBM in this book, but truth be told, when it came time to make a personal computer, they did it right. It has been out about a year and already it is the standard by which all other personal computers are measured.

The keyboard is excellent. The touch is firm and sure. It's detachable, although heavier than most detachable keyboards. As good as it is, the keyboard has two drawbacks. First, the shift key is the size of a regular key, which is far smaller than shift keys usually are. This is compounded by the fact that just below the shift key is a larger key labeled ALT (for Alternate.) It's very easy to hit the ALT, or any other key surrounding the shift key, because of the shift key's smaller size. Further still, the shift key is not located directly next to the Z key, as is the standard, so one often hits the backslash key (which is located next to the Z) rather than the shift key. (Why the inventors of the industry standard "Selectric Keyboard" didn't follow their own standard is beyond me.)

Second, the cursor movement keys are located on the numeric keypad. This means that you can either use the cursor keys *or* you can use the numeric keypad. A special shift key must be depressed to change from one mode to the other. This could prove inconvenient in typing financial statements or documents containing many numbers.

There is an audible and tactile "click" each time a key is depressed on the keyboard. It is subtle, rather like turning a small electrical switch on and off (which, in fact, is exactly what you're doing). Some people find this verification of a keystroke that can be both heard and felt delightful, others find it irritating. You'll have to decide if you fall into the "some" camp or the "others" camp. The keyboard on the IBM personal computer is unlike any other.

The screen is sharp and easy to read. It displays 24 lines, eighty characters per line. The monochrome screen is green phosphor. Graphics are fully supported on the IBM.

The IBM is sold in modular units that allow you to build a system to your liking. A 64K system with two 5¼-inch disk drives (340K per drive), keyboard, and video display would cost around $3,500.

Unfortunately, the 16-bit microprocessor will not run currently available CP/M software without major rewriting.

A solution is known as the Baby Blue Card. (IBM is known in computer circles as Big Blue after, I suppose, the big blue letters that make up its trademark.) This is a card that plugs into the IBM Personal Computer and allows it to run all existent 8-bit CP/M software. It also adds 64K to the memory. It costs $600. This would give one an eight *and* a sixteen-bit machine.

Eight-bit personal computers have a de facto standard operating system, CP/M. Sixteen-bit computers are still battling it out. The two leading contenders are CP/M-86, a version of CP/M for 16-bit machines, and MS-DOS — also known as IBM-DOS. As I'm sure you have guessed by now, a program written for CP/M-86 will not run on MS-DOS and vice versa. Until the marketplace decides the 16-bit personal computer operating system standard, confusion and incompatibility will reign.

The IBM XT

IBM has introduced a color version of the PC, known as the IBM XT. (Would you have believed, even a year ago, that IBM would ever market a product named XT? Sounds like a sports car or an improved mouthwash. How quickly the big guys let their image slip when there's money to be made.)

In its current state, I cannot recommend the IBM XT except for the most narrow of applications. The color video screen produces characters that are far too fuzzy to work with. Processing words and numbers would soon become tedious on this display. If they increase the sharpness of the character display, then this might be an interesting computer. IBM, however, has shown little inclination to improve its PC product. The fact that they still have a non-standard keyboard attests to this. I am not, then, anticipating a sharper display in the near future.

The limited application for the XT would be creating color charts and graphs, and the need to store a lot of them (otherwise the hard disk would not be needed).

Word processing in color, by the way, is a gimmick. Color is totally unnecessary. At some point in the future, when color displays are as sharp as monochrome displays—and as inexpensive—then color might be a useful touch. Until that time, if you want to process words or numbers, think monochrome.

DEC Rainbow 100

In 1960, Digital Equipment Corporation (DEC) set the computing world on its ear by introducing a small computer at an outrageously low cost. Computing power had come within the reach of thousands more. The cost? A mere $120,000.

Today Digital is about to do it again, with a line of small computers that will put computing within the reach of thousands — perhaps millions — more.

These four machines are the Rainbow 100 (also known as the PC100), the DECmate II (also known as the PC200),

the Professional 325 (PC325), and the Professional 350 (PC350).

The one I find most exciting is the Rainbow.

The Rainbow comes with a black & white screen that displays 24 lines of either 80 or 132 characters. (The screen switches easily between the two.) The keyboard is detachable and excellent. It ties with the TeleVideo keyboard as my favorite. (The *my* in "my favorite" is very important — you certainly might prefer others.) The keyboard is detachable. It has a numeric keypad (with add, subtract, multiply, and divide symbols), separate cursor movement keys, and more special function keys than one is ever likely to need (there are 36 extra keys on the keyboard).

The shift key, like on the IBM, is not directly next to the "Z." It is, however, larger than any other keys around it, and adjusting to the new placement is not a major hardship.

The disk drives are double disk drives, each holding two 5¼-inch disks. Each disk holds 400K of information, for a total of 800K.

The Rainbow is an 8 *and* a 16-bit machine. It will run either CP/M or CP/M-86 software. For $250 more you can run programs in the MS-DOS (IBM-DOS) format. 64K of RAM is standard. It is expandable to 256K

The cost is $3,495. Quite a value.

The word processing program chosen by Digital for the Rainbow is Select. I guess we can allow them one mistake. Actually, Select is a good choice for executives who type two letters per week, and maybe that's who they thought would be buying the Rainbow. I am also told the Select offered for the Rainbow is "enhanced." Well, for $595, the enhanced Select would have to be awfully enhanced. In the meantime, it's good to know that almost any word processing program will run, and run well, on the Rainbow.

Digital gives away, for free, a book on personal computing (an embarrassment to those of us who *sell* books at $9.95 per. How would Digital like it if I started giving away *computers* for free?) The book is nonetheless recommended reading for anyone considering a computer — Digital or any other.

On the cover is a photo taken from high above an executive-engineer type, a keyboard sort-of on his lap. The man is looking directly at the photographer with a what-the-hell-are-you-doing-up-there? look on his face. Inside the book, for those concerned about Digital's solvency, is a photo of a building — only slightly smaller than the Great Wall of China — labeled "Digital Equipment Corporation, Parker Street facility."

You can write to them at Parker Street and request your copy. (*Digital Equipment Corporation, Media Response Manager, 129 Parker Street, Maynard, Massachusetts, 01754*) Ask for the book "Guide to Personal Computing."

DECmate II

This is very much like the Rainbow, except the processor is the Digital 6120, which is designed to run Digital's existing word processing program. It is (get this) a *twelve*-bit processor (just when I was getting used to eight and sixteen). But don't worry: for $495 you can have a CP/M auxiliary processor installed and run 8-bit CP/M programs just like everybody else. The CP/M plug-in card also adds an additional 64K of RAM.

The DECmate II, with the word processing software, is $3,245. This would give you a superior stand-alone word processor, for a fraction of the traditional Wang-Lanier-IBM Displaywriter (etc.) stand-alone price.

The word processing program on the DECmate II is powerful and easy to use. It includes dandy features like the display of bold face letters in bold and underlined words underlined on the screen.

For an additional $500 you get a List, Sort, Math, and Communication add-on program that provides sophisticated list management, sorting features, math functions, and a complete communications package.

This is a top-of-the-line word processing program, tailor-made for an excellent machine. It directly rivals the $8,000 to $15,000 stand-alone word processors sold by The Other Guys. (Only a few months ago it *was* one of the $8,000 to $15,000 stand-alone word processors!) It should certainly be considered if you're planning to spend more than $3,500 on your word processing computer.

VICTOR 9000

Victor is a name more commonly associated with adding machines than computers. This is understandable, since the Victor Adding Machine Company has been around almost as long as the Victor Talking Machine Company. Well, the Victor Talking Machine Company became RCA Victor and the Victor Adding Machine Company became Victor Business Products and Victor Business Products has just released an excellent computer.

The Victor 9000 is a state-of-the-art personal computer: 128K RAM, detachable keyboard, 24 eighty-character lines, and two 5¼-inch disk drives, each holding a whopping 620K of information. (Expandable to 1,200K per drive!)

The screen display is the sharpest and, to my taste, most agreeable of any personal computer. Each character is

not only sharp and clear, but is also made up of thicks and thins, very much like a typeface used in printing. The video screen tilts up and down, left and right for maximum operator comfort. The computer has full graphics capabilities.

The keyboard has not only a ten-key numeric keypad, but also a full function calculator. (Well, what would you expect from the Victor Adding Machine Company?) In the midst of any program you can enter the calculator mode, calculate, and then return to the program. This may sound flashy, but a $5.95 handheld calculator glued onto your keyboard would perform essentially the same task.

The Victor 9000 is a 16-bit computer, and all of the current software limitations regarding the IBM personal computer would apply to the Victor 9000.

A company is making a plug-in card for the Victor 9000 that allows it to run any standard 8-bit CP/M program. This $600 card removes my major concern about the Victor: lack of software.

Both CP/M-86 and MS-DOS are included in the price. The price, by the way, is $3,995. Although this is the highest-priced computer in this book, it is also the *most* powerful and, considering the features offered, is a good value. A comparably equipped IBM personal computer, for example, would cost around $5,500. The Radio Shack Model 16, at $5,798, doesn't even come close.

The Epson QX-10

From the picture window of his hillside home, Chris Rutkowski can look North and see the lights of Los Angeles. Chris spends little time contemplating the twinkling of the few skyscrapers in the distance. Most of his time is spent in a small bedroom-turned-office. There he sits with the final prototype of his computer, the Epson QX-10. Chris has a modest goal: From this room and with this machine he plans to alter the face of personal computing forever. The crazy thing is, he just might do it.

The house is alive with new life. Chris and his wife, Joan, have two toddlers: a girl, who wore a Pac-Man T-Shirt; and a boy, who has a Pac-Man belt. In the well-stocked toy room, however, there was not a video game in sight. The boy was busy looking at fish in an aquarium. The girl was playing with a Garfield stuffed animal she had named Ganoosh.

Chris's friend, neighbor and vice president of Rising Star Industries, the design team behind the QX-10, is Gale Carr. She was, as they say, "with child." Very with child. (Late-breaking bulletin from our newsroom: Gale Carr has given birth to a baby boy. Film at eleven.)

Back in 1964 the Seiko Watch Company, responsible for timing the Olympics, introduced an electronic printer. This printer duplicated on paper all those dots used on the large scoring boards to display time, event, and winners. In the past, the journalists had to copy all this information by

hand. Now all they had to do was stop by the Seiko booth and pick up printed copies. The electronic printer (the EP) was quite a hit.

After fifteen years of marketing various forms of the EP mechanism to adding machine manufacturers (among others), the Seiko company decided they would market a printer directly to the American small computer market. The chance of this venture succeeding was slim so, to avoid loss of face in case of failure, the Seiko company named the printer EPSON (EP SON: SON of the Electronic Printer).

In 1980 Rutkowski was the first American hired by Epson America to help market the now legendary Epson MX-80 printer. (As the ads say, with a photograph of Earth in the background, "One company has sold more printers to this planet than any other. Epson.") In two years he sold 150,000 MX-80s. Meanwhile, he was also busy developing his dream computer.

With the blessing and backing of the Epson and Seiko companies, Rutkowski formally departed Epson and founded

Rising Star Industries. The name has nothing to do with Chris's ability to see Hollywood from his living room window. It was a combining of two national symbols: the Rising Sun of Japan and the Stars and Stripes of the United States.

Rutkowski's plan was to combine the unbeatable ingenuity and entrepreneurship of Americans with the superb engineering and manufacturing of the Japanese. The Epson QX-10 is the first child of that partnership.

For many years Rutkowski had been working on a software and hardware combination, the use of which would be so obvious, logical and helpful that no documentation would be necessary. He detailed the specifications of the hardware and turned it over to the Japanese engineers. After many meetings with Rutkowski they returned to Tokyo with a commitment to "try." (Rutkowski: "'We'll try' in Japanese means 'We can do it.'")

He then wrote the documentation and instruction manual, and gave it to his American programmers with the instructions: "Not only incorporate everything in this manual into the software, but incorporate it in such a way that no one but you will ever have to read this book."

So off they went, to different sides of the planet to which Chris had sold more printers than anyone else, to work on Rutkowski's dream.

At one point during his demonstration of his dream-turned-reality-turned-supertoy, he peered at me like Sherlock Holmes posing a new conundrum to Dr. Watson. "What's the difference between bullshit and genius?" he asked.

I could tell by the glimmer in his eye that this was a kind of test, like one Samurai asking another his favorite koan. "Genius is when you get away with it," I replied.

"Very good," he said, and returned to the demonstration.

Chris knows that if he gets away with this project, not only will he have the most wildly successful and widely imitated computer of all time, but he will change personal computers as we know them. They will become, not just "user friendly," but fully accessible, to anyone, without a word of instruction or one page of documentation.

Chris also knows that if he gets away with it, he will be

able to apply his theory of computer design to civilization as a whole. It is true, as Buckminster Fuller said, that Spaceship Earth came without an operating manual. The way Chris Rutkowski would like to redesign Spaceship Earth, it wouldn't need one.

Chris's theory goes something like this: In the evolution of any consumer product, a point of *architectural stabilization* takes place. (An architecture being any collection of design elements.) In 1905, for example, the architecture of the automobile was random.

"Some of those contraptions were steered with tillers like a boat, while others had reins like a wagon," Chris writes. "They had fixed throttles, and throttles on the dash. Some had three wheels. Few, if any, were closed in with a roof. And not one was truly practical for the average person." Drawing a parallel between the automobile of 1905 and the personal computer of today, Rutkowski asks, "Does this sound familiar?"

By 1925, the architecture of the automobile had stabilized. A standard had evolved from 1905 to 1925 that has not changed significantly in the ensuing 58 years, and is not likely to change in the predictable future. All cars have wheels for steering, foot throttles on the right, brakes to the left of the throttle, and one of several standard methods of shifting gears. Most people would have no trouble driving a 1925 Chevrolet, a 1948 Volkswagen, a 1963 Rolls Royce, and a 1983 Chevrolet.

It is time, Rutkowski thinks, for architectural stabilization to take place with personal computers. To this end, he has invented the HASCI keyboard and the Valdocs software system.

HASCI stands for (brace yourself) the Human Applications Standard Computer Interface. (Chris may design computers for the masses, but he still invents acronyms for engineers.) Rutkowski sees keyboards, not mice, as the most effective way for humans to interact with computers. I must say, I couldn't agree with him more. (The mouse, as demonstrated in Apple's Lisa, is good for certain computer tasks but will, I think, always be a secondary adjunct to the keyboard. A mouse is scheduled to be added to the QX-10 at a later date.)

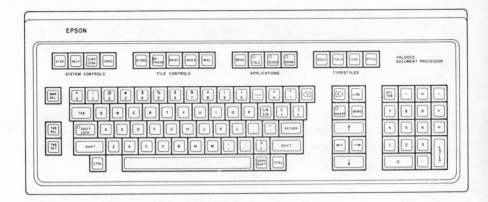

The keyboard must then be laid out in a certain way. A good look at Rutkowski's keyboard will show how well thought-out, how convenient, how (dare I say it?) *user friendly* it really is. After examining a diagram of the keyboard for a while I thought "*Of course* this is how all keyboards should be. It's so...*logical.*"

Examples:

• The cursor movement keys are separate, discrete keys. The Up cursor movement arrow is on top, the down cursor movement arrow is on the bottom, the left cursor movement arrow is on the left, and the right cursor movement arrow is on the right. (In Computerese, by the way, this is referred to as a **North-South-East-West placement** of cursor keys.) "But, of course!" you say. Yes, but look at how many cursor movement keys come in rows (Apple IIe), or are part of the numeric keypad (IBM).

• The numeric keypad includes add, subtract, multiply, and divide keys. Why shouldn't $3,000 computers have all the features of $5 hand-held calculators? I don't know, but very few do.

• There is a single key to delete the character immediately to the left of the cursor. Most typing mistakes are noticed a split-second after they are made. With this key, in one stroke, the computer backs up and erases all that went before, one character at a time. (This is known as a **destructive back-**

space in Computerese.) As useful as this is, it is on less than half of the computers I've seen.

● There is a single key to delete the character you are on, and all characters to the right of it. Handy in editing; missing on most computers.

● There are tab set and tab release buttons. This feature, introduced on Royal Underwood manual typewriters in the late 1940s, is strangely missing from just about every computer keyboard on the market.

● It has two control keys, one on either side of the space bar. This is as useful to touch typists as two shift keys. It also makes the keyboard far more accessible to people who only have the use of one hand. Guess how many computer keyboards have two control keys? This is the first.

Why hasn't anyone put all these logical, obvious (most good ideas are obvious after you've seen them) features together on one keyboard before? My guess is that personal computer keyboards have been steadily improved versions of the old teletype keyboards. These keyboards were so limited (because of the transmission limitations of the telegraph) that they didn't even have periods or lowercase letters. (That's why telegrams in old movies read: "COMING INTO CHICAGO TONIGHT STOP MEET ME AT THE TRAIN STOP BRING THE CASH STOP.")

Chris was simply the first person to look at keyboards with a normal *user* in mind. Most computer designers have looked at keyboards with a what's-been-done-before?-let's-copy-it-and-add-an-improvement-or-two attitude. Someone had to do it, and I'm glad that it's done.

At the top of the keyboard is a row of function keys that, given some experimentation and an occasional push of the HELP key, would allow anyone to copy a disk, do word processing, schedule appointments, perform basic calculations, send and receive electronic mail, and make pie charts and bar graphs *without* having to consult a manual.

And it works.

Of course, the more advanced features of a program would require some written instruction. But to get the computer up and running and doing something productive does not require wading through pounds of documentation.

The software system developed by Chris and his cohorts at Rising Star is called Valdocs (for "valuable documents"). It includes an operating system (TP/M, an improved version of CP/M, but fully CP/M compatible, so I am told) word processing, electronic mail, a calculator program, an appointment scheduler, and a pie-chart-bar-graph program.

It should be noted, however, that the HASCI keyboard and the Valdocs software, while designed to work together, are not mutually dependent on each other. With relatively minor adjustments, any software will work with the HASCI keyboard, and Valdocs will run on any computer.

If, for example, you wanted to use Wordstar with the HASCI keyboard, it would be a simple matter for someone familiar with the Wordstar Customization Notes to adapt the Wordstar commands to correspond with the HASCI keys. If you wanted a more elaborate scheduling program than the one offered by the Valdocs system, pushing the SCHED key would invoke that program. And so on.

This freedom to use programs other than the ones written by Rising Star for the Epson is in marked contrast with, say, the Lisa system. The Lisa and its programs are hopelessly interrelated and inseparable.

The HASCI keyboard is licensable to other manufacturers for the modest sum of fifty cents per keyboard. (This money goes to research grants covering a wide range of subjects.) By charging but a token fee, it is clear that Chris would like to see the HASCI keyboard on computers competing directly with the Epson. In other words, there is no need for other computer manufacturers to reinvent the steering wheel.

As a computer, the Epson QX-10 would be an excellent value even if it didn't have the HASCI keyboard and the Valdocs software.

The processor of the QX-10 is an 8-bit Z-80, and the machine has an astounding 386K of RAM. It has two 5-¼-inch disk drives, each drive holding 276K of storage. The screen is green slow phosphor, exceptionally sharp, and easy to read. It has 25 80-column lines. The screen is also capable of high resolution graphics. The keyboard, in addition to having a remarkable design, has a great touch and is a pleasure to work with. It is, of course, detachable. The overall design (that is, the way the QX-10 looks) is delightful.

The Valdocs word processing software has all the features one might expect from a state-of-the-art word processing program except proportional spacing, subscript, and superscript. It also does not have a spell check program, nor does it have mail merge capability (the ability to generate form letters). All of these features are coming, and should be out in various releases between now and the end of 1983 (with the possible exception of proportional spacing, which may be delayed a while longer). It will also not do footnoting, nor does it offer split screen editing.

Being a CP/M compatible machine, the QX-10 can run any of the currently-available CP/M-based word processing programs. If you have a need for mail merge, for example, you can use any of the programs offering a mail merge option, and later use the Valdocs mail merge feature.

Another drawback is that currently only one letter-quality printer is supported by Valdocs software, the Comrex (which is a Brother printer, distributed by a division of Epson America). Other letter-quality printers should be supported in the near future. (Driving a printer is a function of the software. Other word processing software, run on the QX-10, will drive any letter-quality printer supported by that software.)

A final drawback is one that must be expected whenever any new computer or software package comes along: bugs. To say there might be a few bugs in the software is like saying there might be a few roaches in a New York apartment. The probability is high. (My guess is the only bugs will be in the software. Epson has demonstrated the ability to turn out first-rate, highly reliable products.)

All of these drawbacks are not permanent, and are all software related. Patience in waiting for updates will be necessary for QX-10 users. It is my view, however, that the patience will be rewarded.

The Valdocs software does some things that few word processing programs do. In addition to its ease of learning, it will display bold words in bold on the screen. Also, italicized words in italics. It will even display words in bold italics. (It does not yet display underlining, although that, too, is in the Valdocs future.)

The computer has a clock that remembers day, date, and time—even if the machine is unplugged for shipping. The day and date is automatically added to the index. The index is made up of whatever name you wish to assign your files. No longer are you   limited to one-word descriptions. You can rhapsodize about the contents of a file using, if you like, about twenty words. To find a file, for later editing or printing or telecommunication, all you need remember is any *one* of the words. The computer will display all files with that word in the index.

The computer has some considerate features. For example, if you are working on something you don't want someone else to see, all you have to do is type CONTROL and STOP. This blanks out the screen display until the person has gone. Hitting any key on the keyboard brings back the screen display.

The software also includes a scheduling program (although easy to use, I still think most people will find an appointment book easier), a communications package (easy to use, and well integrated; ex. you can receive a file from someone while editing another), an address book (very handy, in that it will store numbers and dial them automatically if you have an auto-dial modem, and it will also print address labels), a pie-chart & bar-graph program (easy to use), and a calculator (you can go directly to it without leaving whatever else you are working on, and the total can be added automatically to the document being processed). It's an impressive package, with more being added all the time.

The most remarkable thing about this computer, I think, is its price. Not only is it one of the most advanced computers around, with a lot of good software (soon to be great software), but the whole package costs $2,995. (A no-software, CP/M version, with less RAM, is available for $2,495.) This, to my way of thinking, represents a remarkably good value.

The only thing that might keep the Epson QX-10 from

becoming the most successful personal computer since the IBM might be, ironically, Epson itself.

Epson is now large enough to be a bureaucracy, but it has not been a bureaucracy long enough to be a well-oiled bureaucracy. Hence, bureaucratic roadblocks may occur, and, as far as I can see, those are all that might hinder the success of this remarkable machine.

An example of one of these roadblocks has happened with the HX-20. Epson sold these for three months (with heavy advertising) without an manual. That could only happen in a nouveau bureaucracy. A smaller company would make the documentation an A-1 priority and, by God, it wouldn't take three months. A well-oiled bureaucracy would have had the documentation there in the first place.

I mention this, not because I expect difficulty from Epson, but so that you can better understand difficulty with the QX-10 if it arises.

Meanwhile, over at Rising Star, Chris and cohorts are doing what they call guerrilla marketing. No matter *what* Epson does or does not do, they plan to create a demand for the QX-10 that is unprecedented.

Once again, they just might succeed.

PERIPHERALS

I-PROTECT

If you are concerned about radioactive baddies creeping out of your video screen, here is a solution. It's called I-Protect. (The pun I am sure is intentional.)

I-Protect is a quarter-inch thick piece of lead-impregnated plastic. Somehow, they have arranged it so that you can see through lead. The I-Protect screen is, in fact, quite transparent. The lead, however, blocks all of the x-rays and most of the ultra violet rays emanating from the video screen. (This type of plastic is used for windows in nuclear power plants.)

The only problem with I-Protect is that the plastic is about as reflective as the Joy-washed dishes that you can see yourself in. ("And that's a nice reflection on you.") This may be valuable when writing self portraits but, save that, reflected glare is about as troublesome in the short run as radiation might be in the long run.

The I-Protect people are about to solve this problem by laminating a Polaroid filter to the I-Protect shield. In the near future, and for less than $150, you should be able to have the best of both worlds: protection and Polaroid.

I have no idea how real all this radiation danger from video screens is. It will take years of statistical analysis to come to a conclusion. In the meantime, if all it takes is $150 to avoid becoming a statistic, I find that inexpensive insurance. Like my morning handful of vitamins, I may not need any of them during a given day, but I take them anyway, just in case.

Head Head Cleaner

Cleanliness is vital to the correct functioning of disk drives. Not only must the disks be kept free of fingerprints and coffee spills, the read/write heads must be occasionally cleaned for optimum performance.

Head Computer Products sell head cleaning kits that are half the price of everyone else's. A normal liquid head cleaning kit costs about $30. The Head kit is $15. I can't seem to find any difference in quality so, as they say on TV, why pay more?

Dvorak Keyboard Software

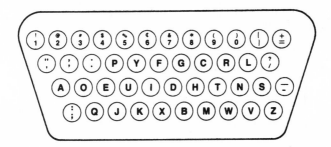

It seems that back in 1873, there was a major problem with typewriters: people typed faster than the machinery could handle. This resulted in a frequent, and annoying, mangling of keys. There was some serious talk of abandoning this newfangled contraption altogether.

Christopher Latham Sholes to the rescue! Chris Sholes did not invent a more efficient typewriter. He invented the *least* efficient placement of keys on the keyboard. He placed the most frequently used letters under the least used fingers. (A and E, for example, under the little and ring fingers of the *left* hand.)

With this intentionally difficult placement of letters on the keyboard, typists seldom overloaded the meager capacity of these early typewriters, and the Machine Age entered the office.

As typewriter mechanisms improved, the keyboard did not change. Mr. Sholes did a good job: his intentionally inefficient keyboard has plagued typists for more than a century.

In the early 1930s, August Dvorak introduced a "simplified" keyboard, one that placed the most often used letters under the most often used fingers.

Following World War II there was a lot of talk

about the Dvorak keyboard, but the typists who knew the old keyboard were, for the most part, unwilling to learn a new one — even one that promised to increase the speed and ease of typing. The Simplified Keyboard fell into disuse.

There has remained a small but loyal following of Dvorak users, much like the Esperantists. One of their main problems was a lack of typewriters. (For the Dvoraks, not the Esperantists.) For a while only Smith Corona made a typewriter with a Dvorak keyboard.

Personal computers, however, might bring the rebirth of the Simplified Keyboard. With the right software, the keys on almost any personal computer can be reprogrammed to conform to the Dvorak standard. Rearranging the plastic keys, by pulling them off and replacing them or by gluing new letters over the old, completes the transformation.

Many people attracted to word processing on personal computers have never typed before. They must learn *some* system of typing: might as well be the Dvorak system as any other. Further, these people are generally not concerned about using their typing as a marketable skill. They are therefore not concerned that learning the Dvorak keyboard will not help them get a secretarial job.

I do not use the Dvorak keyboard. I am a hunt-and-peck typist, and I hear that we are the hardest to retrain. (Touch-typists can relearn the Dvorak keyboard without major trauma, I am told.) The idea of the Dvorak keyboard makes sense, though, and the evidence convincing. Were I learning typing for the first time, I would certainly consider learning Dvorak.

For more information on the Dvorak keyboard, you can send $6 to Philip Davis (*Box 643, West Sacramento, California, 95691*) and ask for a reprint of the article "There is a Better Typewriter Keyboard," and a sample copy or two of his quarterly Dvorak newsletter *Quick Strokes.*

For information on software that will turn your personal computer into a Dvorak personal computer, you can contact Nick Hammond at FBN Software.

D-Cat Modem

When it came time to transmit the text in this book from my computer to the typesetter over telephone lines, a modem was needed. I felt duty-bound to try the least expensive modem advertised, which was $99. If it worked I could recommend it. (Modems are very straight forward. They either work or they don't. Nothing very subjective about them.)

Well, for three painful days I tried to get the $99 modem to work on either of two computers I have. Nothing. The people at the $99 modem company were very nice, but everything they suggested failed to work. (I must have heard the man say, "I can't understand it" more times than I heard Nixon say, "I am not a crook.")

Deadlines were broken left and right. The typesetters were very kind, far more patient than I. Finally I called for help outside the $99 modem company. Brian, my technical ace in the hole, arrived, and plugged in a D-Cat modem. It worked perfectly first time. It has continued to work perfectly throughout the transmission of the entire text.

D-Cat is made by Novation, a company that has been in the modem business for a number of years. They know modems.

The D-Cat is $199. After what I went through with the $99 modem, I can recommend — with not only enthusiasm but gratitude — that you spend twice as much for a D-Cat.

If you plan to make a business out of word processing, you might like to read these two books on the subject.

Peggy Glenn's "How to Start and Run a Successful Home Typing Business" is the bible of work-at-home typists. Although the book does not mention computerized word processing, it is easy to transpose "typing" to "word processing" throughout.

For information about the book, please write to Peggy Glenn, c/o Aames-Allen, 924 Main Street, Huntington Beach, California 92648. (714) 536-4926.

The second is a start-up kit, complete with a disk, tax forms, sample letters and help for the small businessperson in ways (as they say) too numerous to mention.

It's called the "Home Word Processing Service Start-Up Kit" and is available for $29.95 from South Bay Word Processing, 1558 Oro Vista Road, Suite 290, San Diego, California, 92154, (619) 575-8381.

As I mentioned at the start of this chapter, the world of computer hardware and software is changing at a remarkable rate. It's interesting to consider that with all it has to offer, the personal computer industry is less that eight years old.

If you're planning to purchase a personal computer for word processing any time after September 1, 1983, please write and ask for **UPDATE B**. (All other updates have already been incorporated into this text.) It's free, but please enclose a double-stamped, self-addressed envelope.

Peter A McWilliams
Box 69773
Los Angeles, California
90069

Your questions and comments are welcome. Although I cannot promise a personal reply, questions of general interest will be answered and printed in UPDATE ♯B and in future editions of this book, so please write.

Purchasing a Personal Computer

Purchasing a personal computer will, for most people, require visiting a new kind of retail outlet: The computer store. Seven years ago there were no computer stores. Today, they're everywhere.

Please keep in mind that personal computing is in its pioneer days. You'll get along a lot better at computer stores if you treat them like trading posts on the frontier rather than as modern and sophisticated retail outlets.

When spending several thousand dollars on a consumer item, it is reasonable to expect some expert guidance, some personalized attention, and, yes, even a bit of pampering. At a computer store, feel lucky if they open on time.

A couple of years ago, there were only a few computer stores, owned and operated by knowledgeable, well-intended computer addicts who knew how to build, fix, operate, and program any computer in the store. There was only one problem with these people: they could not speak English. They had spent so long in the land of RAM that they were unable to describe life in anything but bytes.

All prospective computer buyer had to do was take a Berlitz crash course in Conversational Computerese and he or she was set. Once you learned how to communicate with the people in the computer store, in their language, you could find out anything you wanted to know.

Then the gold rush came. Someone took a look at the sales curve of personal computers and decided there was gold in them there hills. A great many someones did. Personal computers became the domain of entrepreneurs and investment bankers and venture capitalists and Wall Street. These people were in it for the buck, not for the love of computing.

And so the marketing was turned over to the advertising agencies, store designs to architectural firms, and sales to professional salespeople. These people knew how to speak English, but they didn't know beans about computers. Selling was selling, or so the theory goes, and if these

Taken from "The Personal Computer Book."

people were good at selling widgets, they'd be good at selling computers.

Selling is a skill, just as knowing how to operate a computer is a skill, and I'm afraid there are precious few people in the world of computer retailing who know both. Computer merchandising is growing at such a rapid rate that if a person *did* know both, he or she would wind up as sales manager of the company within six months, *you'll* never see him or her on the sales floor again.

The fact that you will get neither stellar service nor sage advice from computer stores is nobody's fault, really. It would be nice to blame it on corporate greed or laziness or some recognizable evil, but I can't seem to find one.

The computer salespeople I have met are well-meaning and willing to help, they just don't have enough information *to* help.

Look at what they're up against:

1. Computers are changing all the time. If a store sells two or three different kinds of computers, one must know what's currently available, what's planned for in the near future, what peripherals are available, how each of these works, and what they do.

2. Further, one must know what the competition is doing, planning, marketing, and so on. A customer may come in and say, "I saw an ad for The Super Computer in *Time*. Why is your machine better?" A good salesperson should have a good answer.

3. Software is a jungle unto itself. Imagine being asked to know, in even a cursory way, something about every program in a given computer store, much less on the market.

Someone shopping for games might ask, "Do you have the game that's like *Dungeons and Dragons*, except that it has the Red Baron in cell number seven and the green tiger? I played it at a friend's house last week."

Someone shopping for word processing might say, "I need to do script formats, indexing, and footnoting, but proportional spacing is not necessary."

An accountant might ask, "Will this process receivables on a year-to-date or periodic basis?"

And so it would go for every software category. Computer people are not the only ones who have jargon.

4. It would help if the salesperson were a master of psychology. (Ph.D., with a minimum of three years' clinical experience, well-grounded in crisis intervention.) People have the strangest reactions when confronted with a world as unusual and different as computers. For some, the defenses rise to battlestation proportions. Others become so defenseless that they believe anything. Terror, disorientation, hostility. Sometimes it's hard to tell the difference between the waiting room at an out-patient clinic and a computer store.

5. Most people come to computer stores looking not for computers but *solutions*. This and this and this is wrong with my business, my children, and my life. Which machine will fix it, how will it fix it, and what will it cost? For a computer salesperson, the wisdom of Solomon seems to be another prerequisite.

6. Computers appeal to a broad spectrum of people, from pre-pubescents to post-doctoral candidates. A salesperson must be able to discuss programming with ten-year olds and video games with Nobel Laureates. If you're opening a computer store, you might check on the availability of Henry Kissinger.

7. After people spend $5,000 (or $2,000 or $3,000) on something, they expect *service*. "I didn't spend $5,000 on a machine to have it..." People can be awfully demanding.

People write me about **The Word Processing Book** *outraged* that I did not include a review of this-or-that computer, insisting that I write them back at once with my comments. My comments (although I've never dared write them) are that, if they demand that much from an $8.95 book, they'll never get $2,000 worth of satisfaction from a computer, so they might as well give up.

Naturally, the person who must carry the brunt of whatever dissatisfaction the customer might have is the salesperson. He or she must be, in other words, an expert troubleshooter, a crackerjack repair person, and a diplomat extraordinaire.

8. A salesperson also has to deal with the demands of his or her boss and the many manufacturers of software and hardware sold in the store. This takes the patience of Job and the integrity of Serpico.

One could begin to construct a picture, then, of the ideal computer salesperson. If you were to find such a person, you could easily get him or her elected President — or Pope. It is doubtful that, unless you came upon a Saint slumming it for a lifetime or two, this person would be selling computers.

The problem is that it's all so intricate and all so new, and it's getting more intricate and newer everyday. I don't know anyone who has successfully kept up with it all. I certainly don't pretend that I have. People pick an area and specialize: hardware, languages, games. I'm rather fond of word processing myself. You may have to talk to a lot of people in order to capture the gestalt of the whole thing.

There are ways of getting the most out of what computer stores have to offer. Here are some that I have found useful:

1. Make an appointment. Call the store and ask to speak to the expert in the field you are most interested in: accounting, games, word processing, electronic spread-sheeting. All you have to say is, "Which one of your sales-people knows the most about accounting?" When you reach this person, introduce yourself, and make an appointment.

Make it a specific appointment. They may try to get off the hook with, "I'm here every day from nine to five. Drop by anytime." Counter with, "Fine, how about Tuesday at three?" Call in the morning to confirm (i.e., remind them).

With an appointment, you are more likely to speak with the person who knows the most about the subject you are interested in, and you are more likely to get some specialized attention. Not much, but some.

2. Do not be intimidated by jargon. Salespeople who use excessive jargon are either from the Old School of computer selling and know everything about computers and nothing about communication, or they they are from the New School and know very little about computers but are trying to conceal that fact. When in doubt about what a word or phrase means, ask. Asking may not do you any good, but don't be afraid to give it a try.

3. Get some "hands-on" experience. Don't spend a lot of time discussing the philosophy of computing and looking at full-color brochures — sit down at a computer and *play* with the thing. There's plenty of time to talk while you're pushing buttons and watching the results of that button-pushing.

See if you can spend some time alone with the computer. This usually isn't too hard to arrange. When you have enough information to attempt a solo flight, all you have to say is, "Why don't you take care of some of your other customers and come back to me later?" There are almost always other customers to be taken care of.

4. Ask a friend who knows something about computers to come along. He or she will be able to tell you (later) whether the salesperson was giving you solid information or solid, uh, disinformation. They will also be able to, once the salesperson has gone, show you some great things about the computer. (Although don't expect your friend, who runs Program A on Computer B, to know very much about running Program C on Computer B.)

5. Use the computer for what you'll be using the computer for. If you're going to use it for creative writing, write something creative. If you're going to use it for correspondence, write letters. If you'll be doing accounting, do some accounting. If you're going to use your computer as an electronic spreadsheet, bring along some numbers and project some costs. If you're going to play games, play some games.

Different computers are good at different things. One that plays games well may be awful at business, and vice versa.

"What do you mean overdressed? We're going to look at IBMs, aren't we?"

When you're done looking at your desired application, ask the salesperson to show you what else the machine can do.

6. Be on the lookout for good salespeople as well as good computers. If, while in the store, you observe a salesperson who really knows what he or she is doing, and it is clear that "your" salesperson does not, it is time for diplomacy, tact, and trickery. (Going from one salesperson to another is like changing dates after you're at the ball.) First, create some emergency that needs taking care of and leave. (You have to buy your seeds for National Potato Week or something.) The longer you stay in the store, the more the not-so-hot salesperson will feel you "belong" to him or her.

Exit soon, but first find out (a) the lunch hour and (b) the day of the week your original salesperson has off. (Make it sound as though you will rearrange your schedule so as not to miss him or her.) Return to the store next at (a) that hour, or (b) that day. The better salesperson should be on duty, and you now have a new salesperson.

7. Make notes. Write down model numbers, prices, salesperson's names, everything. After leaving the store, debrief yourself and note the pros and the cons of the machines and programs you've just evaluated. The things that are clear in your mind upon leaving a store will be hopelessly muddled a few weeks and a dozen computer stores later. Ask, too, for any printed literature the store can part with.

8. Trust your intuition. It's important that you feel good about the computer you purchase. Include your emotional reactions in your notes and in your decision. Just as cars are more than how many MPG they get, computers are more than how much RAM they have.

9. What happens if it breaks? Be sure to investigate what you'll have to do if the computer does not compute either in or out of warranty. Can you bring it back to the store or will you have to pack it up and ship it to California? How much time will repairs take? Are loaners available for free or at a reasonable cost? Will the store put all its promises in writing? Think about the unthinkable before you buy.

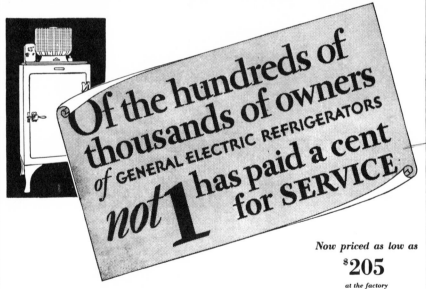

Although personal computers have proven quite reliable, I don't think we'll be seeing many ads like this in computer magazines.

"Now, over here is where we keep the printers."

10. Take your time. Don't try to look at everything in a week. You might experience a Personal Systems Overload. Take it easy. If you must travel to The Big City to do your investigations, it's better to plan several shorter trips rather than one long one. Gather all the information you can, let it digest, and make your decision from a relaxed state of mind.

11. Enjoy yourself. Keep in mind that it's hard to lose. All personal computers have *something* worthwhile to recommend them. To paraphrase Father Flanagan, there are no bad computers. You might not buy the best computer that fills your every need for the best price, but such is life. Whatever you do buy will serve you faithfully, teach you several magnitudes more about computers and computing than you know now, and assure that your next computer purchase will be an almost perfect one. Knowing there's no way to lose, enjoy playing one of the most intricate and challenging computer games around: buying a computer.

In getting the best price on your personal computer, it pays to shop the back pages of the various computer magazines (*BYTE* in particular). There you will find mail-order companies that sell computers at rather remarkable discounts. Some computers will be there, and some computers will not. Different computer companies have different policies, and although "fair trading" (i.e., price fixing) was ruled illegal some years ago, some companies control their dealers such that you can be sure you will never find one of their products sold for less than full retail price.

If the computer store in your area offers absolutely nothing in the way of knowledge and support, or if you live a goodly distance from even the closest computer outlet, you might consider buying a computer by mail. Most mail-order computer companies have good reputations, but the unspoken agreement is, "We'll sell you a computer cheap, but you're on your own after the sale." That means that fixing the computer is between you and the manufacturer (most are good at mail-in warranty repairs), and that learning the computer is between you and the Almighty.

"Don't be afraid. There's nothing in a computer store to harm you."

If the computer store in your neighborhood seems to know what they're doing, can communicate that with a fair degree of intelligibility, and seems to be able to offer you after-the-sale support (a repair department, software, peripherals, maybe even classes), then buy from them.

You may or may not be able to get a lower price from the local computer store by showing them the ads in the magazines. They may give you a special "systems price," or throw in some software, or offer to come over to your house and set it up. Most stores, if they are interested in your business, will make some concession somewhere.

Don't expect them, however, to "meet or beat" the price in the mail order ad. The unspoken agreement between you and a walk-in computer store is that they will be there to serve you after the sale. This costs something, quite a lot actually and, like a club, you pay your dues when you join.

You might, too, consider hiring your salesperson, or someone you met in your quest for RAM, as a consultant. This is especially true in a business environment. Offer them $25 per hour — or more — to review your computer purchase just before making it, set the computer up, test it out, make sure everything is working, teach you (and your staff) how to run different programs, and be on hand to answer any questions as they arise (and believe me, they will arise).

If your consultant works, say, ten hours at this task, he or she might prove to have been the most valuable $250 peripheral you could possibly have purchased.

This brings us to an end which is, really, just the beginning. (Be careful. I tend to wax poetic and sentimental at goodbyes.)

It's been my pleasure escorting you through a small portion of this maze known as personal computing. I hope I have been of some help.

Happy computing!

An Illustrated Guide to Selecting and Purchasing a Personal Computer

Taken from "The Personal Computer Book."

*More and more people are discovering the joys of personal com-
puting every day.*

Those who have not taken ample time in selecting their computer have had reason to regret it.

Get the advice of those who have trod the path of computer ownership.

Be sure to read good books on the subject.

Weigh the advantages and disadvantages of each computer system carefully.

Don't overtax your system by getting one too small to meet your needs.

Be sure to read good books on the subject.

Investigate the reputation of the store from which you plan to purchase your computer.

People who sell computers on street corners and back alleys are seldom reputable.

Find out if the purchase price of your computer includes delivery and set-up.

Be sure to read good books on the subject.

And even if you haven't read any good book on the subject, be sure to ask the advice of someone who has.

Be open to good advice from any source.

Even with expert guidance, it's easy to get in over your head.

After visiting a number of computer stores, you might want to go through the collected business cards and see which salesperson you liked best.

If you play your cards right, you'll wind up with a computer you can be proud of.

The author with his first word processor
Christmas, 1956

About The Author

There's little point in being coy and writing a biography in the third person. "Peter A McWilliams was born in Detroit, Michigan..." That sort of thing.

I was, indeed, born in Detroit, Michigan in the summer of 1949. My first writing was at the age of four. It was more plagiarism than writing. I faithfully copied the squiggles and wiggles in a book I found, having no idea what any of it meant. I showed it proudly to my parents.

Thinking I had authored the piece—no mean feat, as I had not yet learned to write—mom and dad were favorably impressed. It was, in fact, the most enthusiasm shown me by my parents since the arrival of my younger brother one long year before. Why for even a moment they thought I had written, "Scarlett O'Hara was not beautiful, but men seldom realized it when caught by her charm as the Tarleton twins were." is beyond me.

After learning I did not originate the piece they were duly disappointed, but it was too late. Somewhere in my four-year-old mind I decided to become a writer, and the rest of my life fell into place.

My love of the written word was such that on Christmas, at the age of seven—when most young boys were petitioning Santa for baseball bats and football helmets—I begged for, and received, a typewriter: my first word processor.

I self-published my first book in 1967. I was seventeen. There were two books actually, a gathering of love verse and a collection of poems on society. The love poems sold better. They sold so well, in fact, that a few years and a few thousand books later I had become, "The best selling poet in America under thirty."

And then, in the same dark month, I became thirty *and* I learned that Richard Thomas (John-Boy Walton, for heaven sakes) had sold more poetry than I. For a while I toyed with the idea of billing myself as, "The second-best selling poet in America under thirty-one," but decided eventually upon, "One of the best selling poets in America."

There are currently nine volumes in the poetry series in print, and they have sold more than 2,500,000 copies.

In 1975 I co-wrote and published **The TM Book**. This rode the popular wave of interest in TM to the top of the *New York Times* bestseller list, where it remained #1 for four weeks. Ours was the first book in more than a year to surpass **The Joy of Sex** in sales. I was expecting the headline "TM is Better Than Sex," but it never came.

In 1976 I revised—-with a psychologist and a psychiatrist — an earlier book I had written. The earlier book, published in 1972, was called **Surviving the Loss of a Love**. The expanded edition I published as **How to Survive the Loss of a Love**. It still sells 8,000 copies per month.

After a disastrous attempt to publish a line of greeting cards, I repaired to California for a few years to lick my wounds. It was there that I studied at the feet of the silicon masters and learned all that I know about word processing—almost all of which is in this book. **The Word Processing Book** is my first book — other than poetry — to be published since **How to Survive the Loss of a Love**.

The publication in late 1982 of **The Personal Computer Book** earned me the title (bestowed by *The Houston Post*), of "The Dr. Spock of Personal Computers." My word.

All of the above adventures are painstakingly detailed in my autobiography **In Dubious Talent**. It has yet to be published. It has yet to be written. Finding the time to write these few words was difficult enough. Without my trusty word processor I never would have attempted it.

The author extols the virtues of word processing to an attentive AT&T board meeting

Addresses

Here, in no particular order, are the addresses of the manufacturers mentioned in this book.

Apple Computer
10260 Bandley Drive
Cupertino, California
95014
(408) 996-1010

Otrona Corporation
(Makers of the Attache Computer)
4755 Walnut Street
Boulder, Colorado 80301
(303) 444-8100

TeleVideo
1170 Morse Avenue
Sunnyville, California
94086

Smith-Corona
65 Locust Avenue
New Canaan, Connecticut
06840
(203) 972-1471

Radio Shack
Fort Worth, Texas
76102

Epson America, Inc.
(Epson dot matrix printer)
3415 Kashiwa Street
Torrance, California
90505
(213) 539-9140

Sony Corporation
(Typecorder)
Office Products Division
9 West 57th Street
New York, New York
10019

Heathkit Electronics Corporation
(Heath H-89)
P.O. Box 167
St. Joseph, Michigan
49805

Zenith Data Systems
(Zenith Z-89—-assembled
version of Heath H-89)
1000 Milwaukee Avenue
Glenview, Illinois
60025

Xerox Corporation
Stamford, Conn.
06904
(203) 329-8700

Atari, Inc.
1265 Borregas Avenue
Sunnyvale, California
94086
(408) 745-2213

Interface Age
(Magazine)
P.O. Box 1234
Cerritos, California
90701

Non-Linear Systems
(KayPro II)
533 Stevens Avenue
Solana Beach, California
92075
(714) 755-1134

DynaType
(Computerized typesetting from
word processors through modems)
740 E. Wilson Avenue
Glendale, California
91206
213-243-1114

BookMasters
(Book printers)
830 Claremont Avenue
Ashland, Ohio
44805
(800) 537-6727

Xedex Corporation
(Makers of Baby Blue for IBM)
1345 Avenue of the Americas
New York, New York
10105

WP News
(A word processing newsletter)
1765 North Highland #306
Hollywood, California
90028

Commodore Computer Systems
681 Moore Road
King of Prussia, Pennsylvania
19406

BYTE
(Magazine)
P.O. Box 590
Martinsville, New Jersey
08836

North Star Computers, Inc.
14440 Catalina Street
San Leandro, California
94577
(415) 357-8500

Oasis Systems
(The WORD, The WORD Plus,
Punctuation and Style)
3692 Midway Drive
San Diego, California
92110
(619) 222-1153

Lifeboat Associates
(Software distributor)
1651 Third Avenue
New York, New York
10028

Ring King Visibles, Inc.
(Makers of disk storage files)
215 West Second Street
Muscatine, Iowa
52761
(800) 553-9647

MicroPro International
(WordStar and other software)
1229 Fourth Street
San Rafael, California
94901
(415) 457-8990

Peachtree Software
(PeachText and other software)
3 Corporate Square
Suite 700
Atlanta, Georgia
30329
(404) 325-8533

JMM Enterprises
(They sell adapters
  for the Osborne)
P.O. Box 238
Poway, California
92064
(714) 748-8329

Novation
(Makers of the D-Cat modem)
18664 Oxnard Street
Tarzana, California
91356
(800) 423-5410
(In California: 213-996-5060)

Discount Software
(Software at Discounts)
6520 Selma Avenue
Suite 309
Los Angeles, California
90028
(213) 837-5141

Dover Publications
(Publishers of the
Dover Archive Series)
180 Varick Street
New York, New York
10014

Select Information Systems
(Makers of Select and an
interactive tutorial on
how to use CP/M.)
919 Sir Francis Drake Boulevard
Kentfield, California
94904
(415) 459-4003

NEC Information Systems, Inc.
(Spinwriter letter quality printer)
5 Militia Drive
Lexington, Massachusetts
02173
(617) 862-3120

Muse Software
(Word processing for Apples)
330 North Charles Street
Baltimore, Maryland
21201

Victor Business Products
(Victor 9000)
3900 North Rockwell St.
Chicago, Illinois
60618

The Source
(Data Bank)
1616 Anderson Road
McLean, Virginia
22102

CompuServe
(Data Bank)
Available at any Radio Shack
Computer Center

Personal Computing
(Magazine)
4 Disk Drive (cute, huh?)
Box 1408
Riverton, New Jersey
08077

Creative Computing
(Magazine)
Box 789-M
Morristown, New Jersey
07960

Aspen Software
(Grammatik)
Box 339
Tijeras, New Mexico
87059
(505) 281-1634

Information Unlimited Software
EasyWriter II
281 Arlington Avenue
Berkeley, California
94707
(415) 331-6700

IBM
Information Systems Division
Entry Systems Business
(I have no idea what the
last six words mean)
P.O. Box 1328
Boca Raton, Florida
33432

Popular Computing
(Magazine)
P.O. Box 307
Martinsville, New Jersey
08836

WordPlay
Document Processing Center
(They rent word processors
  by the hour)
9037 Melrose
Los Angeles, California
90069
(213) 859-1221

Cromemco
280 Bernardo Avenue
Mountain View, California
94043
415-964-7400

Small Systems Engineering
(CP/M Card for Victor 9000)
1056 Elwell Court
Palo Alto, California
94303
415-964-8201

Toshiba America
Information Systems Division
2441 Michelle Drive
Tustin, California
92680
714-730-5000

Eagle Business Systems
28362 Marguerite Parkway
Mission Viejo, California
92692
714-831-8810

Jonos Ltd.
(Escort)
920-C E. Orangethrope
Anaheim, California
92801
714-871-1082

Dynax
(Distributor of
Brother printers)
333 South Hope Street
Suite 2800
Los Angeles, California
90071

Digital Equipment
  Corportation (DEC)
2 Mt. Royal Avenue
Marlboro, MA
01752

Osborne Computer Corporation
26500 Corporate Avenue
Hayward, California
94545
(415) 887-8080

Daisywriter
3540 Wilshire Blvd.
Los Angeles, California
90010
213-386-3111

Franklin Computer
(Makers of ACE 1000)
7030 Colonial Highway
Pennsauken, New Jersey
08109
609-488-1700

Bytewriter
125 Northview Road
Ithaca, New York
14850
607-272-1132

Digital Marketing
(Micro Link II)
2670 Cherry Lane
Walnut Creek, California
94596
(415) 938-2880

Lexisoft
(Spellbinder)
Box 267
Davis, California
95617
916-758-3630

FYI
(SuperFile)
Box 10998
Austin, Texas
78766
512-346-0133
800-531-5033

Innovative Computer Products
(Perfect Data Head Cleaner)
18360 Oxnard Street
Tarzana, California
91356
213-996-4911

Langley-St. Clair
(I-Protect Radiation Shield)
132 West 24th Street
New York, New York
10011
212-989-6876

Sanyo
51 Joseph Street
Moonachie, NJ
07074

Sony Microcomputer
   Products Division
(Sony Computers)
7 Mercedes Drive
Montvale, NJ
07645

Hewlett Packard
1430 East Orangethorpe Avenue
Fullerton, California
714-870-1000

Lanier Business Products
1700 Chantilly Drive Northeast
Atlanta, Georgia
30324
800-241-1706

FBN Software
(Dvorak Keyboard Software)
1111 Saw Mill Gulch Road
Pebble Beach, California
93953
408-373-5303

Lifetree Software
(VolksWriter for IBM)
177 Webster Street
Suite 342
Monterey, California
93940
(408) 373-4718

Screenplay Systems
(Scriptor)
211 East Olive Avenue
Suite 203
Burbank, California
91502
213-843-6557

Perfect Software, Inc.
(Perfect Writer)
1400 Shattuck Avenue
Berkeley, California
94709
(800) 222-4222

Morrow Designs
(Morrow Micro Decision)
600 McCormick Street
San Leandro, California
94577
415-430-1970

Teleram
2 Corporate Park Drive
White Plains, New York
10604
914-694-9270

Dictronics
(The Random House Thesaurus)
362 Fifth Avenue
New York, New York
10001
(212) 564-0746

InfoWorld
(Computer Newsweekly)
375 Cochituate Road
Box 880
Framingham, Massachusetts
01701
(800) 343-6474

NuKey
Business Solutions, Inc.
91 West Long Lake Road
Suite 14
Bloomfield Hill, Michigan
48013
(313) 540-3360

TVI 2000 Conversion
Word Tech Systems
Box 7005
Lafayette, California
94549
(415) 254-7747

Smartkey
Heritage Software, Inc.
2130 South Vermont Avenue
Los Angeles, California
90007
(213) 737-7252

123
Lotus Development Corporation
Cambridge, Massachusetts
02138
(617) 492-7171

Word Proc
Roger Hagan Associates
1146 Fairview
Seattle, Washington
98109
(206) 628-9673

Head Head Cleaner
Head Computer Products, Inc.
Tarzana, California
91356
(213) 342-9600

The Zorba and The Nomis
Telcon Industries, Inc.
1401 N.W. 69th Street
Ft. Lauderdale, Florida
33309
(305) 971-2250